Metaphorically
SPEAKING

Metaphorically SPEAKING

REFLECTIONS ON HAPPINESS, SUCCESS, AND OTHER FICTIONS

ALLIE POTTS

Axil Hammer Publishing
2021

Copyright © 2021 by Axil Hammer Publishing
All rights reserved. This book or any portion thereof may not be reproduced or used in any manner whatsoever without the express written permission of the publisher except for the use of brief quotations in a book review or scholarly journal.

First edition
ISBN 978-0-9968320-6-9

Ordering information
Special discounts are available on quantity purchases by corporations, associations, educators, and others. For details, contact the publisher.

U.S. trade bookstores and wholesalers: Please contact Allie Potts at
www.alliepottswrites.com

For Tori, who helped me find the humor in almost every situation, or failing that, an excuse to nap.

Contents

Introduction	i
Names Found in This Collection	1
Faking It 'Till You Make It	4
The Lesson of the Tooth Fairy	9
On the Lookout	13
Lavender Fields	17
A Day at the Beach	23
Double Down on Good Company	26
A Night Out With My Prince	29
Let it Snow	33
Enough	38
Please Forgive Me	42
The Magnolia Tree	46
Dangerous Perfection	49
Celebrating the Storm	54
For Those Who Think I Have It All Together	58
The Invention	63
No Signal	68
The Reading	73
The Tale of the Improbable Boat	77
The Place Where the Sidewalk Ends	81
Persistence	86
Changing Parameters	89
Resolutions	92
Contemplating Success at the Corner Bus Stop	96

A Bump in the Night	101
When Life Is Determined to Get In Your Way	107
Impostor Syndrome and the Fear of Success	113
Jeopardy	122
Marathon Strong	125
Adventures in Goal Setting	134
Mountain High	138
Harder, Better, Faster, Stronger	142
Friendly Neighborhood Spider-Man	149
Life Isn't a Spectator Sport	153
One Foot Forward	157
Get a Grip	162
The Tale of Two Vines	166
How I Almost Lost My Feet to Save My Face	170
An Unexpected Lesson on Never Giving Up	175
Fly Robin Fly	179
When All is Said and Done	184
Bonus Stories	189
Acknowledgments	209
About the Author	211
Other Titles by Allie Potts	215

Introduction

Early in my writing journey, I came across a bit of advice: before you put the first word to page, think about something you believe in and the rest of the words will come. Well, I believe that we as a society have allowed for too much negativity in our lives. We are controlled by the idea that we are not good enough, don't have enough, somehow might be found to be less, which creates a ripple effect on the next generation.

I am fascinated by the psychology of happiness, however, I am not a licensed medical professional. This book is not for someone who is suffering from clinical depression or other clinical mental disease. I firmly believe in the benefits of medicine and that there is no shame in seeking professional treatment. I didn't put this book together as a substitute for either of those things.

However, I knew that at one point I had allowed myself to become dissatisfied with my general day-to-day. I also knew that I had no reason to be. I had a good-paying job, a nice house, a growing family, but I couldn't help thinking it wasn't enough. *I wasn't enough.*

I've since become much different (and dare I say a better) person today than I was back then. To be clear, it wasn't easy. I didn't just wake up one morning and say, today is the day I will be happy, or worse—stop trying. No, it took time and a combination of regular reaffirmations, positivity, and mindful thinking to change my perspective. The mindset adjustment also isn't permanent. You have to work at it constantly. This is something that really proved to be the case during the stress of COVID lockdowns.

The following is a collection of musings I've jotted down over the span of five years. These are not arranged in chronological order. This was intentional, as it allowed common themes to better shine through. As a result, my children may be in school in one story, and diapers in the next, but then again they will always be my babies in my mind's eye, even when they are full-grown with children of their own.

I enjoyed putting this collection together. In my case, it proved to be especially beneficial to remind myself of these moments during the lockdowns of the pandemic, but that wasn't the reason I started this project. This collection of my everyday experiences exists because I am a storyteller and hope that they might inspire others to find their own path to happiness one day at a time.

Everyday
STORIES

Names Found in This Collection

I once came across a discussion in an online group on how authors select names for their characters, and I found it to be a rather interesting discussion. I fall into the category of people who think that the meaning behind a name is an important consideration. Not just when creating fictitious characters for a story, but in all things.

For example, one of my sisters met a woman who was joyfully describing how she had selected a unique sounding name. When asked to spell the name out, my sister learned the woman had inadvertently given her new daughter the name of a sexually transmitted disease. I will grant her that the young girl is probably not going to come across very many others with the same name in her life span, so if unique is what the mother was going for, she achieved it. Poor girl—if only her mom had done a quick reference check. I believe her mother thought she was naming her daughter after a flower.

When naming our sons, my husband only wanted to make sure that the names had a family connection. If someone in our shared ancestry had been called a name before, that was good enough for him. I, on the other hand, researched each and every name for its linguistic origin and meaning. I also took it a step further and verified their potential initials for negative connotations. I also researched to see if the combination of first and middle name matched historic figures with questionable reputations. I even tried to pick a name that's meaning spoke to both the Roman and Chinese Zodiac characteristics of their anticipated due dates.

Okay, so looking back, maybe I took the selection of a name to the extreme.

As it turned out, my older son was several days late. His astrology chart no longer lined up with my well-thought plan. I could have, and likely should have, saved myself the effort. Kids . . . for being as small as they are, they do create big messes.

Perhaps I should have gone with a colleague's method. She, a mother of four, suggested all I need do was pick three names that sound good together when you are shouting. The tip comes in handy, especially when you find yourself yelling for your child to pay attention for the tenth time.

That said, the names I used regarding my various friends and family members throughout the following pages are as fictitious as the names of the characters in my books.

Faking It 'Till You Make It

We took a quick road trip over the weekend. As per usual, the boys demanded a movie within seconds of the engine starting. We kept a pile of DVDs ready for just such an emergency, but we'd played them so many times the hubby and I could repeat the dialogue by heart, and were, therefore, not exactly thrilled to fire up the player. We told them they were going to have to wait until we reached the interstate.

The entertainment system also came with two sets of headphones so that backseat passengers could listen to their movie while the front seat listens to the radio. Unfortunately, my youngest was only two at the time. This meant he had no interest in keeping a large electronic accessory strapped to his head.

My eldest, being only slightly more mature than his brother, was patient for approximately ten minutes. I'm sure it felt like hours to him. He begged us once again to turn on a movie. We told him we would put the movie on after his brother fell asleep. He immediately turned to his brother and said, "go to sleep so we can watch a movie."

If my youngest was any older, I am sure that would have been exactly the wrong thing to say to achieve his goal. Instead, my youngest smiled and pretended to fake sleep, including snoring. Snoring loudly. Then not so loudly.

I turned around. He had pretended he was asleep until it became his reality and was slumped over in his chair. I handed over the headphones to my eldest and fired up the DVD player. Three out of four of us achieved our goal.

The moral of the story is sometimes you have to fake it to make it. Or in my sons' example, have your underlings fake it until you make it.

Mark Twain once said that "to succeed in life you need two things: confidence and ignorance." The ignorance part is easy. We all start out as amateurs. Had I known everything I know now about a number of things, would I have taken the same path? Maybe. I can't say, but I wouldn't be the person I am today had I not veered off course or made a mistake or two hundred.

The confidence part is trickier. How can you build up your confidence if you've never done something before?

Some people take issue with the phrase fake it to make it as the word fake implies that what you are doing is deceitful and or a lie. I understand where they are coming from, but I fear that they may be getting caught up on the literal definition. You should never commit fraud or portray yourself as anything other than authentic, but adults can and should still play make-believe. Like a toddler mimicking the actions of an adult, or older sibling, you have to act in the manner in which you believe a successful person should act.

It's not brainwashing. It's practice.

In this manner, you gain experience, which reinforces belief. Belief then fuels confidence. If you can convince yourself that you deserve to succeed, then one day you may just discover that you are no longer pretending.

I've considered and reconsidered the definition of success, as it relates to me personally, over the years. Sometimes more seriously than others. When asked during a job interview, I once gave the cheeky answer: it was to never eat Ramen Noodles again (I have yet to achieve that one). However, I realized that while economic comfort was important; it is only a component of success, not the complete definition.

I've since concluded that success to me now means being happy with myself and what I surround myself well. Unfortunately, I've also realized that a success based on economic comfort alone might be far easier to achieve.

This is because there is no one magic formula for happiness—no fairy visits you in the middle of the night, waves her wand, and magically transforms you into a newer, better version of yourself. It takes work and constant effort. Happiness is hard, because we, as a society, have allowed it to be, but luckily, this is a learned behavior and if we can learn it, it can be unlearned too. You can start by changing your perspective.

When I started my examination of success and happiness, I looked for inspiration and saw my children. I couldn't help noticing their world consists of home, school, daycare, and the occasional visit to Nana's or a cousin's. Some might consider their world small. And yet, to them, it is something wonderful and worth exploration. I started writing the lessons about life my children taught me.

I became more aware of the moments. By putting my observations down in writing, I recalled the lessons my parents, grandparents, and even husband taught me—wittingly or otherwise, and as I did so, I developed a deeper appreciation of them. Not just for how they have supported me, but as individuals as well.

This is not to say that since starting this process, every day has become rainbows and lollipops. They haven't. That's life. But I've found it far easier to be happy when you surround yourself with other people who are happy. Therefore, I have chosen to share my stories, in the hope that they might inspire you to take another look at your own everyday and, maybe, just maybe, help change your perspective. After all, a little change is good for us all.

The Lesson of the Tooth Fairy

Speaking of small change, I'm reminded of the first time the tooth fairy visited our house. We'd known the visit was imminent, but even so when it came time for my son to lose his first baby tooth, he didn't give her a ton of notice. The tooth, itself, was loose and gone within the same day. Afterward, my son nearly broke the sound barrier getting ready for bed that evening eager to see whether the tooth fairy would come.

The following day, he reached under his pillow and pulled out a shiny quarter. He gave us all a great big gap-toothed smile and placed the coin in his bank. He then proceeded to call my attention to the gap repeatedly and made sure that all his friends at daycare were equally informed. In his mind, there could be no more solid proof that he truly was a big kid now.

I informed my extended family and co-workers about this recent development, only to learn that the tooth fairy had gotten off incredibly cheap at our house. Apparently, inflation affects more than just the cost of a gallon of milk.

In case you are curious, I've since learned that the going rate for a child's tooth is actually a dollar or more on average. They often cited five dollars for a first tooth or larger tooth, such as a molar.

My son was excited to receive his quarter. He'd never asked the tooth fairy upfront how much she thought his tooth would be worth and was thrilled. All he had expected was a coin, and a coin is exactly what he received. But it worried me all the same.

This is because when my son is excited about something, he likes to tell everyone who will listen all about it. At the time, there was a genuine risk that he would talk to an older child at the playground about the receipt of his quarter and learn that the other child received more. If that happened, would his joy suddenly be turned into shame? Would he wonder to himself things like why didn't he receive more? Why wasn't the tooth fairy just as generous with him? Was there something wrong with his teeth? Was there something wrong with him?

We often confuse self-worth with financial worth. However, if you were to ask most business owners, they would tell you that money is actually one of the worst ways to incentivize your staff. Monetary bonuses tend to provide little positive long-term impact on employee behavior and typically result in the exact opposite of their intent.

People adjust to bonuses. They start to expect them and become dissatisfied doing their regular work when they don't receive them. Company culture can also take on a climate of unhealthy internal competition depending on how the bonus is structured. This is why studies have shown that companies that pay a fair wage and offer other benefits designed around the values of the employees are more productive than companies that offer barebones salaries with astronomical bonus potential.

There is an alternative to this system called the prosocial bonus. The concept is simple. Rather than cut a check to an employee in reward for the job they should be doing anyway, the employee gets to redirect where the bonus goes. The only catch is the funds must go to some place other than their bank account. An employee might request money be spent on a cause of their choice or on their teammates. While it may not seem motivational on the surface, studies have shown people respond well when being given a chance to be a decision maker even if they don't get to keep take home a monetary benefit. They get to feel empowered.

In fact, companies who have experimented with the concept reported their employees had a greater sense of self-worth, even though their financial worth wasn't adjusted. This created a culture of increased morale and teamwork. However, I need to point out that the system only works if a person is paid fair wages in the first place. I also digress.

This brings me back to my dilemma—what to do about the tooth fairy's short-coming.

I dug the quarter out of my son's bank. Luckily, upon examination, my son and I were able to ascertain it still had residual fairy dust. I explained to my five and a half-year-old, all he had to do was behave himself all day, make a wish while holding the quarter near his tooth gap, and place it in a cup of water for the magic of the first lost tooth to work. The quarter grew overnight into a silver dollar. He may have just gotten his first lesson in investment, as he had to move his money into a different vessel and do a little extra homework for it to grow.

Thankfully, we managed to avoid an awkward discussion about disparity. While a little change might do him some good, at this point in his life, I am sure he would tell me a lot of change would do him even better.

On the Lookout

*H*owever, change isn't always pleasant, nor is it always small. I was in college on September 11th, 2001. Most of my family was hours away, including a cousin, living in Brooklyn, who no one could reach. Several hours later, I learned my cousin had gone into town after hearing about the first crash, never expecting there to be a second crash or that the towers might come down.

My cousin was okay, but as I listened to reporters say how the world would be forever altered, all I could think of was those other people who had gotten on a plane that day or had gone into work thinking September 11th was going to be no different from September 10th and my heart went out to those they left behind. Just as it does to all those affected by any tragedy, even those that play out on a less international stage.

Tragedy teaches us that every day is precious.

The world has gotten none less scary, but it doesn't have to stay that way.

Fred Rodgers, the host of one of my mom's favorite children's shows, once said that as a boy, when he would see scary things in the news, his mother would say, "Look for the helpers. You will always find people who are helping."

She was right. For every tragedy, there are stories of regular people who ran into danger instead of away from it to save others.

These everyday heroes create hope that good will ultimately prevail. Their stories can rally a community and strengthen it. We just have to remember to look for the right story.

After I told my family that I wanted to try writing professionally, one of the best pieces of advice I came across was to identify one thing that you wholeheartedly believe before you write a single sentence and then develop your story around that premise.

Well, I believe that while I have plenty to complain about, I have more to be grateful for. I also believe that every day has value. Even the bad ones—as long as you keep your eyes open.

I was reminded again of this at a much more mundane time in my life, years later. My day job sent me to a communication and presentation-speaking training. As it happened, my group was tasked with giving a speech on something we felt passionate about as part of the coursework.

It could be any topic. The goal was to have high energy and require the use of loads of gestures. I am passionate about a number of things, but put on the spot, I found it difficult to think of anything I would be comfortable sharing with the group. I considered my husband's business. He owns his own company, so in my household, we know only too well what can go wrong for your business when you hire the wrong person for the job. Unfortunately, the words I might use to describe all the specific ways in which I knew this to be true weren't work appropriate.

Luckily, I didn't have to go first.

One of my colleagues walked to the front of the room and gave a speech on how it is important to find the win every day. She provided several examples. Getting through multiple green lights in a row was a win. Issuing a quote to a new customer was a win. Contacting a hard to reach client was a win. Hearing an unexpected thank you for a job well done was a win.

The definition of the day's win wasn't important—all that matter was that an achievable win exists every day. The win should be something that makes the day special. Something small that made the day worth experiencing.

She reminded me in that quick speech that there is always something you can cling to even on your worst days, provided you open your mind enough to recognize the win for what it is. Her speech helped break me out of my own internal stress cycle, recognize that the past was done and it was time to return my focus to the present. It was proof once again that not all heroes wear capes.

Lavender Fields

The experts say that planning a vacation does a better job of reducing stress than the vacation itself. I believe it. As much as I've looked forward to experiencing new scenery, the physical act of traveling to another destination has caused much heartburn and more than one cold sweat and upset stomach.

Years ago, my husband and I planned to visit my family's ancestral home, located just outside of Dubrovnik in Croatia along with my parents and my sister. None of us lived in the same city, but we found flights that were expected to land around the same time, even if not on the same airline. Once booked, I spent the next several weeks worrying about what to pack and how to communicate once there, but hardly thought about the logistics of getting to our destination.

"Canceled? What do you mean canceled?" we asked an attendant as we stood, stunned, at the ticketing counter on the day of the flight with our bags in tow.

"You should always check ahead," the agent muttered. We felt it best not to respond.

The agent sighed before offering, "let me see what I can do." Click. Clack. Clickey, clack. "Okay, I can get you on another connection . . . hmm . . ." Click. Clack. Clickey, clack. "Yes, I can get you on an earlier flight, through Vienna by way of London, but you'll need to hurry."

Bags checked, we rushed to the security checkpoint along with several dozen other passengers headed to other destinations. At the sight of the line, I panicked. I knew my family's flights were already off the ground. They wouldn't know how our plans had changed—I hadn't thought to sign them up for alerts. I looked at my ticket, the other passengers, and at the large digital clock. "Ma'am," the TSA agent caught my attention. "Ma'am, you are going to need to calm down or we aren't going to be able to let you through."

Calm down? Calm down? Did my near breathless panting as I ran up to the checkpoint not clue him in that time was not on my side?

Fine. I took a deep breath, attempting to appear serene. I'm sure I failed, but at least we could enter the line for the first leg of our now four-leg journey.

On the second leg, I watched as the graphic meant to represent our plane on the in-flight entertainment system showed us approaching London. And passing London. And approaching London again. Psst, the flight's overhead speaker system spat as it came online. "Ah, Ladies, and Gentlemen we've been told that there is a lot of ground congestion. We're going to need to circle around a few more times while the runways clear, but don't worry, we'll get you on your way soon."

I glanced at my ticket and at my watch. It would be tight, but there was time to make our next connection. There just had to be.

An attendant stopped by our seats, dashing my hopes. "You aren't going to make it."

What do you mean we aren't going to make it? I started rummaging through the seat pocket for the vomit bag. I was going to need a vacation after this vacation.

We wouldn't finally reach Dubrovnik until the following day. Thankfully, I'd found my phone allowed for international text messages, even if it wouldn't make calls, so at least my parents weren't equally frantic when we didn't show.

After a long cab ride from the airport to Old Town Dubrovnik, I was stressed and travel weary. All I wanted to do was put my feet up. Unfortunately, the downside about visiting a walled city recognized as a World Heritage site is the distinct lack of accessibility by modern transportation. It dismayed me to learn the only way to reach to reach the home we'd rented was by ascending several flights of narrow stairs while carrying our bags. My back and calves ached. No part of this vacation was going to plan.

Eventually, though, it was time to locate something to eat and the group of us followed the rings of stone footpaths and more stairs until we'd reached a line of open-air restaurants. We sat back and waited for our order. And waited. And waited some more. No one seemed to care about turning over a table so that other patrons might eat. Who runs a business like this, I wondered?

The owner approached our table. Rather than apologizing for the delay in bringing out our food, he pulled out a bottle of a locally distilled beverage and offered us a glass freely, as if we were visiting relatives rather than customers. My dad and hubby tasted it, but one whiff of its strength was enough to tell me I was better off abstaining. The owner told jokes as the food was brought out and made sure we all felt welcome. Apparently, a happy one, I answered myself.

Mealtimes the following day played out similarly in both informality and length. Each meal drug out so long that by the time they served us, there was really only time to plan where to eat next. I had heard of the slow food movement, but this went beyond what I had experienced at various trendy tapas bars in the States.

Dubrovnik is a cruise boat destination and during the prime season they crowd the streets of Old Town with tourists, but the season was nearly over. The streets were filled instead with lavender in the form of soaps, oils, and as a featured ingredient in bottles of an otherwise clear beverage similar to the one from the night before, but what was missing was a sense of pressure. If you were interested in one of the various wares, you bought something. If you weren't, there was minimal attempt to persuade you otherwise. It was as if they were content to let life work out the way it would.

We ventured outside of Dubrovnik to where my family's house still stood in a state of mid-renovation. In the distance, I could see tufts of wild lavender scattered across an otherwise rocky hillside. Their presence explained the plethora of lavender based products in the market below. I watched as tall blossoms, where little else grew, undulated in the wind like the waves of a purple ocean. I was one of the most beautiful scenes I have ever witnessed.

Later, as I sipped on a cup of coffee in an open-air plaza while watching the people go by, I thought to myself how lovely life was at that moment and felt the last of my stress go. Eventually, I knew I would have to return to my home and all of its rushing from "a" to "b", but that was a problem for another day. For the balance of my trip, I was content to simply be like the fields of lavender and the people who had built their livelihoods around it, and let the wind take me where it would. And that was a souvenir worth taking back with me.

A Day at the Beach

I needed a break from the heat, and maybe a few other things I am beginning to associate with June. We headed to the beach with my family and my sisters' families for some much-needed rest and relaxation (or as much as you can expect when you are traveling with seven kids 10-years-old and under and three dogs).

We'd picked out the home shortly after the new year. That had been a whole stressful process in and of itself, requiring lengthy negotiations and more than a few compromises, but it checked the major boxes. It had beds for us all—or so the ad claimed, with a pool as well as an oceanfront view and beach access.

On paper, it was perfect.

In reality, not quite. The beach access was not directly across the street as it had appeared in the photographs and at some point, the owners had replaced bunk beds with queen-size meaning several of the kids would have to enjoy even more cousin time, but it served its purpose.

We arrived in mass with cars loaded up like the opening credits of the old show Beverly Hillbillies. All that we were lacking was our family matriarch riding in a rocking chair up top (she'd wisely driven separately). We divided rooms and filled the cabinets with a week's worth of groceries while the cousins darted around and attempted to keep watch of the various canines.

The first day was great. The second too (the nights—not so much). However, storms rolled in mid-week and the combination of early-week sunburns, over-tired small people forced to share beds, a flare-up of a stubborn ear infection, and more than one instance of a pup bolting from the house and very nearly becoming a decorative hood ornament on a passing car, caused my sisters to consider calling it a week early.

I chose to stay the duration and volunteered to watch a couple of my nieces on the beach while their parents packed. Sunglasses on, book nearby, and beach chair out, I prepared to soak in the last rays of stress-free (or at least stress-lite) living. It didn't last long.

A niece marched up to me, crying. Her eyes stung. Hastily applied sunscreen had mixed with saltwater, rendering her blind, and in pain. She couldn't see or swim. The sand was no fun. She wanted to go back to the house, and she wanted to go now.

I looked over my shoulder. I could see the house over the dunes. We hadn't been gone nearly long enough for my sister to pack their stuff away and clean. I did the only thing I could. I handed her a towel. She complained her eyes still hurt. I grabbed a bottle of freshwater and instructed her to tilt her head, while I splashed her face.

"Now dab," I said.

"Dab?" she asked.

"Yeah dab," I said again, gesturing at the towel in her hands.

"Okay . . ." she replied. But instead of drying her eyes, she lowered her face and swung both arms out, parallel to each other, in pure celebratory fashion.

In short, she dabbed.

I couldn't help it. I cracked up. Leave it to the younger set to take a perfectly good simple instruction and interpret it in a way you'd never see coming.

It might have been the freshwater rinse. It might have been the trendy move, but in either event, the smile returned to my niece's face. She returned to the others where they built sandcastles in the surf until noon.

It wasn't a perfect trip, and it's been far from the perfect summer, but moments like those proved that there are still plenty of reasons to laugh, even with things aren't as expected.

Double Down on Good Company

We were invited to join my husband's Rotary club for its first annual casino night. Proceeds from ticket sales would go to charity and outreach, but I was looking forward to it mostly as an excuse to glam up and throw the children at the mercy of a babysitter. Gambling is technically illegal in the state of North Carolina, so instead of using actual money, they gave each guest three $100 bills (bank of Milton Bradley) which could then be exchanged for plastic chips at the table. We could then turn chips of a certain value in for raffle tickets (it's the economic circle of life); the grand prize being a flat-screen TV.

The room was packed with card tables and eager players. After dazzling one dealer with my grasp of the rules of Texas Hold'Em (by 'dazzling' I mean irritating and by 'grasp' I mean a complete lack thereof) I wandered to a table more my speed. Blackjack. The cards just have to be closer to twenty-one than the dealer's without going over. No bluffing. No double blinds. Just simple math with a dash of luck.

My mom, who was also attending the event along with my sister and their respective spouses, had been playing for a while as I settled into an open spot at her table. Mom's game is Bridge, and within seconds it was clear that she was as equally out of her comfort zone playing Blackjack as I was at the poker table. This dealer, Joe, didn't seem to mind playing teacher as well as cards (Mom is adorable when she is clueless). A casual suggestion or nod of his head, and Mom was soon winning about as much as anyone else at the table. My sister joined us as Mom went on a hot streak. Others noticed. They really didn't have a choice. We were loud. We laughed. We teased. We had a great time.

After what felt like a minute, the emcee announced we were nearing the end of the night. By this time, my luck had come and gone. Joe looked at Mom's hand. "You want to double down," he stated more than asked. I peered over at her hand too. She had already bet practically everything she had. She didn't have enough to double her bet. I looked at my cards and my remaining chips. But I did.

I placed a $100 chip (my last) beside hers. "She doubles down!" I said.

"No," she looked at me in shock. If we lost, I would be out of the game. I would have to spend the remaining evening watching others enjoy their fun from a distance.

"Why not?" I answered (In Mom I trust). Her expression, as she realized I was willing to risk it all for her, was worth the cost of our ticket.

The final cards were dealt. Joe displayed the house's hand.

"Winner!"

The three of us jumped up and down, shouting with excitement as Joe slid the winnings her way (tween girls at a boy-band concert have nothing on us).

We didn't walk away with the TV that night (neither of us really needed one anyway). Instead, we walked away with an evening that will go down in the family's history. Some people will describe a house of cards to be one that is weak or one built on a shaky foundation, but in our case, the cards strengthened our family, and a well-deserving civic group gained guaranteed attendees for next year's event.

A Night Out With My Prince

*I*t had been more than fifteen years since I'd gone on a date with anyone other than my husband, but one Saturday afternoon I found myself looking forward to doing just that.

I made sure to pick out a dress that was sure to please. A combination of slacks and a nice blouse just wasn't going to do. As I came down the stairs, my date was already there, and I took satisfaction in the smile that broke across his face.

"Mom! You are a pretty princess!" he exclaimed.

In his next breath, my son amended his comment. "Well, you aren't green dress pretty (his favorite of my outfits) but you are still pretty." My son was quick to give praise at the age of five-going-on-six, but was also great at finding ways to keep me humble.

I was taking him to see a local live theater production of Disney's The Little Mermaid. It was an evening showtime, but even so, at least a third of the audience was made up of children close to his age. Nearly all of them were female.

As the play progressed, I wasn't surprised that some changes were made for the stage adaptation. However, I didn't expect that the big climatic sequence at the end would be one of those edits. The prince no longer drove a jagged piece of shipwreck into the sea witch, saving the mermaid from certain death. No, in this version, the mermaid saves herself as well as the king. In fact, the prince is entirely absent from the climax.

The witch is defeated, and Ariel and her father have a heart to heart. Only then does the prince reappear. Additionally, in this adaptation the prince spends the majority of the play contemplating abdicating his crown for a life as a sailor, and only accepts his responsibility when Ariel emerges victoriously from the waves with her very muscled father behind her. I will admit as the curtain fell, I felt ill. Sure, it was a great play for the girls in the audience, but what about the boys? What message was it sending?

I regularly attend networking functions with other working moms and other executive women. Often there are discussion prompts such as 'what is the one thing you hope to pass on to your daughter' or 'what are you doing to empower the next generation of women in the workplace?' While I appreciate the thought process behind these prompts, they always bother me. Did I betray my gender by only having sons? Is there no place for young boys in a 'Girl Power!' world? I refuse to accept this.

I wish more boys had been at the performance. It was a special night out with my son that at least I will remember forever. He held my hand both to and from the theater. He curled up in my lap during the love songs and proudly proclaimed to our seatmates how happy he was to be there with me. Other mother/sons missed out on a truly magical bonding experience. Why? Because it was a musical play about a princess.

My sons love their LEGOs, transformers, toy backhoes, and front loaders. They love to play in the sand/dirt, fight pretend bad guys, and build things with tools. They are about as stereotypical boys as they come. However, my sons also like cooking, painting, and reading. They are just as likely to play with the kitchenette set at daycare as they are the train table.

I may not have daughters today, but I may, in the far, far, far, (did I mention far) future have a daughter-in-law. For now, I am raising my sons to be just as confident running a household as they are a boardroom, so that if they do choose to stay home for the betterment of their family, they can do so without feeling like their masculinity has in some way been threatened. I am raising them to be respectful of women beyond using proper manners. I am raising them to understand that women can do anything, but at the same time I am making sure that they know they can too. If I am successful, my sons will hire, promote, or feature a woman because she is the most qualified or most deserving, not because she is a woman and certain standards have to be met. That is how I am empowering the next generation. That is the gift I intend to pass on to my future daughter—may she be equal to my son.

Let it Snow

The year 2020 finally ended. I say finally, because though years historically have ended after midnight on the thirty-first of December, without fail, this particular year seemed to be filled with more drama than one might expect within a single three hundred and sixty-five days (or three hundred and sixty-six days, if it is a leap year) period.

This seemed to be especially true as the year wound down to its last days. Each week presented a crazier and crazier new story. The meme creators, who'd joked about the writers going all in on the 2020 season finale, proved to be prophetic. So much so, that I have to admit I considered that the once far-fetched theory that we were all living our lives in a simulation much like the plot of the movie, The Matrix, may not be so crazy after all. I mean, I write fiction on a semi-regular basis, but even I wouldn't have ever dreamed up some of the headlines. Orcas were going on the offensive, attacking ships. Scientists discovered that there could be a hole in Antarctica leading to another dimension. Aliens have not only been in contact with us for decades, we've been denied application into the Galactic Federation—a former government official from Israel said so! And let us not forget about the growing threat of murder hornets, which I still feel is a plot point that has yet to be resolved. All real stories from 2020.

Unfortunately, life did not instantly return to normal following the stroke of midnight on New Year's Day. We were no Cinderella, and the year some twisted ball. No, the headlines continued though the calendar year had changed. January 6th, 2021 happened.

I stood at my desk and watched in shock as the events played out over the streaming newscast. My children, who had been learning at home off and on since March of the prior year, worked in the adjacent room. I ran out to them to let them know what I was witnessing. "Rioters have broken into the Capitol Building!" I told them in a state of stunned amazement. It was clear from their expression that the words rolling off my lips made about as much sense to them as they did to the person who spoke them—albeit for different reasons.

"It's the Capitol," I said again, as if the second telling would make it more comprehensible. "People are inside."

My boys shrugged and turned back to their lessons.

I suppose I could have, should have, made this into a teachable moment. Both boys had studied the basic branches of government already as part of their school curriculum. Political ads had filled the space between their favorite TV shows relentlessly for months. They knew that there had been an election. They also knew that those elected weren't yet sworn in. Their grandfather has served in local politics. We're well aware how the cycle works.

Instead, I returned to my office and finished out my business day as best I could with the news playing in the background.

It turned out, my experience was not unique in my family. My cousin reported a similar story out of her home. The only difference being when she made a comment about how she could not believe what was happening, her son acknowledged his mother was speaking. He said, I know you are shocked, but from my perspective it is just another Wednesday.

The alarming thing about her story was that her son's statement wasn't an exaggeration, even though he was in his first year of college. Life had been this way for a while.

Oh sure, a year ago we could still eat inside of restaurants and only those who lived in the eastern hemisphere wore masks when they were sick—a remnant practice from the SARS outbreak of 2001. However, there had been near-weekly school shootings, and scandal after scandal. People were dying, others were lying.

Unfortunately, it would seem that the childhood I enjoyed does not seem to be the same one these later generations are inheriting. It makes me wonder how we allowed ourselves to reach this point. Why is it accepted that the tail-end of my generation, and the one that immediately follows, will be the first to be worse off than our parents? Was there some deal offered before we were born that gave us carefree summers of playing outside until the streetlights came on with no adult in sight or the opportunity to ride in the back of a car with no seat belt at the expense of certainty of our mature years?

If this is the case, does that mean that our children's experience will be the opposite? Were they more canny bargainers? Did they agree to sacrifice their youth for the freedom of a grand utopian future? Or will they still be paying for the mistakes of their short-sighted predecessors?

I would like to say the former, and yet, as the weeks of 2021 progress, I am afraid my optimism may be the equivalent of a modern day fairy tale.

I am afraid, but I am not willing to give up. With each passing day, I have grown ever more determined to do my part to ensure that while the news on the television might be frightful, the sense of family in the room is delightful, and since we have nowhere to go . . . my children will be as prepared as they can be when it snows, even if the shovels are only metaphorical.

Enough

One of the greatest benefits of entrepreneurship is the feeling of being completely in charge of your own destiny. You get to make the decisions. You are responsible for your business' success. This feeling is great, as long as things go according to plan. But when have things ever gone according to plan?

Employees might get stuck in traffic, or not show. It might snow, shutting your source of income down for days. Suppliers might go out of business, leaving you scrambling to find an alternate. Customers might decide at the last minute that they would be better off going with the competition. Then, being in charge is stressful. It is up to you to make sure your company does what it promises it will do, delivers what and when it says it will.

For that reason, I was okay when the hubby announced he was going to have to work late one night, hoping to close a deal over two years in the making. We are a team. I would solo parent for the evening so he could do what he had to do. It was no problem. Except, every now and then it is.

I collected the boys as I typically did at that time. My eldest was six and had recently discovered Pixar's Wall-E. He decided the balance of the car ride home was the perfect opportunity to hone his robot impression. His was pretty good, but I felt he really nailed it on the second try. He certainly didn't need the twenty something follow-up attempts. Why mess with perfection?

I then arrived at daycare to collect my youngest, who was three, only to be informed he hadn't been feeling like his chipper self that day. He was complaining of a tummy ache. My gut clenched up. My work week was filled with meetings, and several were from visitors from out of state. Of course, he would be coming down with something.

I saw the empty spot where my husband parks in our driveway. Suddenly, recalling his statement that he would need to work late, I felt very much alone.

My eldest decided he didn't feel like bringing in his school things. My baby didn't feel like eating. Six insisted on playing with a loud helicopter toy next to the phone while I attempted to talk to their dad. Three didn't want to go upstairs for his bath, wear the pajamas I had picked out, or pretty much anything at all that he hadn't first instigated. It was a long night of adulting.

The next morning, the hubby needed to sleep in. He hadn't gotten home until well into the morning hours. I realized I would be on my own . . . again. I rushed around the house trying to get both boys ready as quietly, but as quickly as possible. "We are going to miss the bus! ¡Ándale! Mach Schnell!" I said. English clearly wasn't getting through to my boys—I had to mix it up. *Ugh*, I thought, glancing at the clock, no time to pack a lunch for myself. I was already late. What a way to start my day . . .

As I frantically herded them through the door, my six-year-old asked me, 'Mom? Why are you so mad?'

The question stopped me in my tracks. Was I stressed? Absolutely. Did I need to be? Absolutely not. If I would have stopped focusing on all the reasons, I should be stressed and taken a second to look around I might have noticed that my eldest had helped pack his bag that morning. My baby had willingly worn everything I brought him and had tip-toed so as not to wake daddy. Both had helped put their dishes in the machine after breakfast. They were pitching in as they were able. They reminded me that while I might be the only parent awake; I wasn't alone. We were in this together.

What if I was a few minutes late, or didn't have a packed lunch? We'd somehow survive, but I might never get this time with my children back.

The past and the future can be equally blinding. When you fixate on either, you risk failing to see what you need to do in the present. I stopped. I took a breath. I told my boys I wasn't mad, along with a thank you. They might think I was thanking them for their help, but I was really thanking them for the reminder to be mindful of the present. When I told them I loved them, they smiled and hugged me back. For that moment, it was enough.

Please Forgive Me

AN OPEN LETTER TO MY DOG:

We pulled out your crate this week, unused for the last three years, and brushed off the cobwebs, only we didn't do it for you. Another four-legged creature joined the family and needed a place to sleep. I think you would have liked her. She's a mix of Lab, like you, but Boxer too, which was always your favorite playmate. But she's not you.

Then again, you might find her strange. She doesn't chase after cats, or squirrels, or stare at a mysterious nothing in the room's corner, making my neck hairs rise. When we go on walks, I don't worry my arm might be torn from its socket due to the strength of her pulls. She doesn't jump on arriving guests, or feel the need to defend the household from the threat of the evil vacuum. Nor does she enjoy running in front of my shins as I attempt to descend the stairs just to ensure I'm paying attention.

People we meet keep telling me she is perfect. But she's not you.

You would be proud of the boys. How well they've adapted to an animal in the house once again. They grin and tell me how happy they are to have her. They've helped me bathe her, comb her fur, and brush her teeth. They're teaching her to fetch and sit and shake. She's so patient with them too. The boys have draped themselves over her body and used outside voices near her ear, and yet she still she wags her tail at their arrival.

We tried to make you proud of us as well. She is a rescue like you were once, but an older pup. We estimate she's around four years old, but with signs that suggest those years weren't always easy. When we met her, Kiddo announced proudly that we hadn't found her, she had found us, echoing the words I once used myself to describe our first encounter with you.

Your dad tells me our family feels complete once again. But she's not you.

She's smaller than you were, but only just slightly. She is tall enough that I can scratch her head with my fingertips without bending over, but light enough for me to carry when she is feeling particularly stubborn. She has a pink leash and collar, which would have appalled you were you not color blind, but she doesn't seem to mind. She just seems happy to have found a family.

The other night, after the boys had gone to bed, she hopped on the spot on the couch next to me and laid her head on my lap the way you used to do. Soon I found myself growing tired as I listened to her rhythmic snore. I glanced over and saw tan fur where there once lay black, and I had to blink away the tears of my surprise. In my weary state, I'd almost forgotten it wasn't you. I thought I was ready, but it hit me so hard—just then—how much she's not you. In that moment, I realized how different a brain's readiness can be to one's heart's.

I felt so guilty. Guilty that I was enjoying her warmth by my side. Guilty that we couldn't do more to keep you there longer. Guilty I am happy to once again see a bowl on the ground.

But she really is a good girl, and I was the one to suggest we bring her home. In fairness to her, I am trying to remember all your flaws as much as I recall your virtues. How you could clear the room after a meal. The books of mine you destroyed. That incident with the bunny.

The trouble is, I loved you with your flaws as much as you loved me with mine.

I remember those early puppy weeks before you were house-broken, and the pain inflicted on my arms by your needle-sharp teeth and all the reasons we chose not to adopt a puppy this time. I remember wondering if we'd made a mistake back then, injecting your brand of chaos into our lives as I surveyed the damage that once was my living room. But mostly I remember how much we grew to love you over the years that followed. If the decision to bring you home, back then, was a mistake, it was the best mistake we've ever made.

She's only been with us a few short days and is getting to know us as much as we are getting to know her. She's not you, true, but she's herself; a dog who is sweet and mostly well-mannered. A dog who deserves to be loved for who she is rather than considered somehow flawed for who she's not.

So please forgive me if I eventually allow my heart to stop comparing, as difficult as that seems now. When I scratch her behind her ears or throw her a ball to chase, it doesn't mean I miss you any less. It will just mean I've finally allowed my heart to grow more.

The Magnolia Tree

𝒥 took the dog for a walk. The act wasn't particularly notable. I haven't yet been confined to the house for an extended period, or otherwise recovering from some debilitating injury or illness. This isn't a story of bravery. It wasn't cold outside, nor was it overly hot. This isn't a story about overcoming the elements either. In fact, there was very little about that morning's walk that might differentiate it from any other walk I might take on a given day. But on this average walk on an average day, for whatever reason, I happened to beyond the space where my feet came in contact with the sidewalk.

I saw a tree in a neighbor's yard. A magnolia, to be exact. Its blooms had taken on the yellowish tone of petals past their prime and the leaves were already showing signs of summer browning. It wasn't a beautiful specimen, but it wasn't remarkably ugly either. The best word that I can use to describe it is, average. Being that we naturally prefer to seek out that extraordinary, my eyes immediately sought something more interesting to look at and landed on the more wooded area behind the magnolia where trees more than twice the magnolia's height swayed against each other in the breeze. In comparison, the average magnolia now looked isolated and puny. It looked almost as if it wasn't even trying.

I felt a little sorry for the tree as I compared it with those behind it. I remember a magnolia tree in front of my childhood home that seemed to touch the sky. I remember climbing its thick branches, pretending to set up a home well above the ground like Tarzan or the Swiss Family Robinson, and using its huge strong leaves as a fan in the summer. When I was a child, there was no grander tree than a magnolia. It made me pause. To think, I was now considering this magnolia tree small and weak when the tree in my memory had achieved so much more.

The trees that towered behind average magnolia did not grow to their massive heights overnight. With so many close together fighting for the same sunlight, they had no choice but to grow up with each new generation building upon the last growing ever so taller. That kind of success takes time as much as determination.

As I continued my walk, I imagined what the other trees might say to the average magnolia were they to talk. (I know, it might sound odd, but that's the sort of thing that crosses my mind especially early in the morning). Did the other trees look down on their tiny neighbor in disdain, confident in their combined successful heights like some stereotypical A-list high school clique? Or did they secretly envy the shorter tree for the wide-open space around its branches as they tangled theirs with their neighbor's?

It occurred to me then why the magnolia tree had stopped growing upward. It didn't need to reach the same heights as its neighbors to be successful. It grew where no other trees did, spreading its branches out to collect sunlight where little competition existed. The average magnolia had achieved an entirely different sort of success.

It reminded me of a quote attributed to Napoleon Hill: "The strongest oak of the forest is not the one that is protected from the storm and hidden from the sun. It's the one that stands in the open where it is compelled to struggle for its existence against the winds and rains and the scorching sun.

And so, as I finished my loop around my block, my thoughts about the magnolia tree also came full circle.

At the end of the day though it doesn't matter if a tree grows up or out. To be successful, all a tree has to do is to grow a little every day. The same applies to people too.

Dangerous Perfection

*I*n college, I took an introduction course into nuclear engineering. As part of the class, we visited a small reactor owned and operated by the university. Within the facility stood a deep tank filled with water required for regulating the reaction. A series of lights embedded in its walls illuminated the entire tank making the water glow like a sapphire in the sun. Besides the striking color, I also noticed how still the water was. Its surface wasn't marred by a single ripple. I'd never seen anything like it. I thought it was beautiful. I wish I had taken a picture, but the people operating the facility weren't fans of that idea for some reason.

The professor warned us to stay back. The water was beautiful, but it was dangerous. However, it wasn't radiation that we had to worry about.

In order to maintain a controlled reaction, the water in the tank had to be absolutely clear of all minerals or other imperfections. As my professor explained, if we were to fall into the tank, no amount of kicking or flailing of arms would slow your descent. It didn't matter if you were born part fish. You could not swim (or float) back to the surface. To float, you must be able to displace mass. Your body needs those minerals to push against to move through the water.

The water was deadly because of its perfection.

I no longer pursue perfection. I am not saying that I don't always try my best. I just now better appreciate my limitations. I've learned that some of my 'flaws' might actually help to keep my head above water.

There are nooks and crannies where dust bunnies hide on my floors and corners where cobwebs still hang. All this means is that I've gotten a jump on my Halloween decorations. There are days in which there is more work to do than hours in the day. On those days, I could burn the midnight oil trying to do everything myself and still fail. Instead, I recognize that I have colleagues who are more than capable of sharing the load. In fact, and this one is hard to admit, there are some tasks that others are actually more capable of completing than I am. I don't have to do it all.

I don't want to do it all.

By admitting to myself that there are just some things I don't care about, by admitting there are things others can do better, I've found I can focus more on my family and my true priorities. Instead of stressing out about being the best that I could be, I am learning to be content with being the best me, flaws and all.

Flash forward a few years, I was rather unexpectedly sent to Chicago on behalf of the day job. Now, most of the time I like Chicago just fine, but it was January, and the kids had been sick. Saint Augustine may have once said, "The world is a book, and those who do not travel read only a page," but I would argue who isn't guilty of occasionally wanting to skim a page or two every now and then? In short, the timing of this trip was less than ideal.

As we began our descent, the pilot announced the weather had warmed to a balmy 20 degrees (-6C). *Darn, and here I'd forgotten to pack my bathing suit.* Upon arrival, I huddled with other passengers in a what was essentially an airlock while we waited for the airport shuttle to arrive. When the shuttle finally arrived, I almost missed it entirely as the hotel branding was nearly hidden behind a sheet of salt and gray sludge.

I checked into my hotel and made my way into my room. The air inside was only a few degrees warmer than the outside. At least there wasn't a wind chill. I glanced at the window mounted heater box, curious as to the thermostat setting. I expected someone turned it down, what I didn't expect was that someone turned it off all together.

Chicagoans really don't notice the cold. I immediately corrected this problem, cranking the heat up, but even so I knew would take a while for the little heater to make a difference.

Burrowed under my covers, I couldn't quite escape the chill. I wound up passing that night with my gloves on and my winter coat draped over my shoulders. If images of the Poor Little Match Girl running through my head weren't incentive enough to stay awake, the various loud noises coming from the adjacent room helped.

The following day, I told a colleague all about the accommodations from the night before. He cocked his head and asked why I didn't complain about the room to the hotel management. I should have, in his opinion, been given an alternate room, or at least be charged less for the experience. I suppose he was right. He should know, after all, his job takes him on the road at least five to ten times more than mine.

Why hadn't I complained?

Like most people, I do tend to indulge in a bit of self-reflection at the beginning of the year, and this year has been no exception. And yet, I still haven't completely figured out the answer. Was I silent because I feared confrontation after a long travel day? Was it because I am female, and if studies are to be believed, biologically conditioned to accept pain and discomfort, provided it is only temporary? Was it my sense of self-reliance? I had gloves and a coat in the room. Why make the fix someone else's responsibility when I can do it myself?

Or . . . and this thought gave me significant pause . . . after working on improving my outlook for so long, had I learned to accept too much.

I'm a big believer in accepting you can't have it all. After all, who'd want to when you really think about it? That said, there is a difference between acceptance and settling. Our imperfections can be lifesavers, but there is still a value in fighting back when it matters. Therefore, it is important to know where that line is. I've accepted my flaws. I can't park a car in the lines. I can't cook a chicken through the first time, but I've told myself I can't accept is a threat to my family's health, safety, or happiness. I just have to remind myself from time to time that 'my family' should also mean me.

Celebrating the Storm

The first hurricane of the season of 2014 brought high winds, rain, and a bit of flooding on the coast, but was mostly a non-event. North Carolina is no stranger to this sort of weather and it usually takes more than a category-one storm to really get our attention. However, even if a storm isn't strong enough to warrant evacuation, you really shouldn't venture outside through its duration. Even short gusts of more than sixty miles per hour winds are enough to fell a weakened tree or transform a bit of debris into a missile.

Therefore, it is a regular part of the Southeastern experience to spend several hours, if not days, stuck inside your home out of a sense of precaution in at least once a year from June until November as well as when the snows (or more commonly ice) falls in winter. It is a conditioning that should have made it easier to accept the lock downs, when they eventually occurred six years later, but I supposed even a champion runner who mastered the art of the sprint, can be no match for a marathon.

In any event, it is common practice to throw what is known as a hurricane party around here during these times of street closure. This event is much like any other party. There can be excessive drinking except a hangover the following day is the least of your worries.

You can surround yourself by friends and loved ones, and be having the time of your life. However, at the same time you may be scared to death of the force of nature surrounding your four walls. The wind makes its presence known. Unless you've really given in to the adult beverages and cranked up the volume on the music, thoughts enter your head—especially as you grow older. What if the boards or tape on the windows aren't enough to prevent the glass from breaking? What if your insurance doesn't cover flood damage? What if everything you've worked so hard to build comes crashing down in a single instant? Eventually these parties aren't nearly as much fun as they once were.

Peak hurricane season is also the start of the school year. When my eldest son entered kindergarten that year, I admit I was a little apprehensive. Until that first day, he had been cared for in a small preschool class taught by a woman who loves him almost as much as her own children. We'd prepared him for elementary school as best we could. He knew his letters and numbers. He could read his sight words, follow directions, and play well with others. There would even be a graduation party with cupcakes and other goodies made to celebrate what a wonderful boy he had grown into.

But as much as it overjoyed us to celebrate his accomplishments (and the end of half of our preschool tuition checks), I was nervous. He's enjoyed a sheltered existence. He was king of his class. While his new school was highly recommended, he was going to be one of many. I didn't know if he would be able to win over new friends and teachers with his charm, or if he'd have to learn how to get by without favored treatment. We are all going to make more than a few adjustments.

I recognize I could have elected to keep him at home. The homeschool program has come a long way in recent years. There are several people I know who have used it successfully, but even then, there would be no guarantees that our lives in the long run would have been made easier. We would merely experience a different set of challenges.

Up until that point, I'd been able to plan everything for him. What he wore, what he ate, when he slept, and who he hung out with. However, school meant he'd have a chance to start making a portion of those decisions himself. This meant that while he was learning things like reading, writing and arithmetic over the next several years, I would be forced to learn a lesson of my own. I would have to learn how to let go.

It may be somewhat chaotic. He will make mistakes, but he'll be able to learn from those mistakes. I have to accept that letting go will help us both become stronger, better people.

I can speculate what the future might hold for my son. I can lose sleep from worry. I can hold my breath at pick-up until I am blue while I wait for him to tell me how the day went. Or I can send him off, full of hope and excitement, knowing that we've prepared him as best we were able for his life's next chapter, confident that we will find a way to deal with whatever life throws at us later down the line.

I can worry about things out of my control tomorrow or I can raise my glass and celebrate today. I can do any number of these things, but what I can't do is stop the years from turning. I would have as much luck halting the advance of a hurricane.

For Those Who Think I Have It All Together

INSPIRED BY *ALEXANDER AND THE TERRIBLE HORRIBLE NO GOOD VERY BAD DAY*

My boss came into my office. "I am going to throw a curve ball at you," he said, shutting the door.

Just like that, I could tell that it was going to be a terrible, horrible, no good, very bad day.

"Kay has turned in her notice."

Kay was one of my peers. This announcement meant there was a better-than-average chance a portion of her work would find its way to me, at least temporarily, while the position was refilled. I looked at my mug. "I am going to have to start spiking my coffee," I replied while I considered moving to Australia.

My boss laughed but didn't disagree.

Yep, I could tell it was going to be a terrible, horrible, no good, very bad day.

Five o'clock rolled around, ending an office day filled with sympathetic looks and panicked responses (many of which were mine). I raced out the door. My husband was out of town the rest of the week (a trip I hadn't known about until the afternoon before), therefore it fell on me to pick up our children from their various locations. All I had to do was get there on time.

I hit traffic.

Much later than I'd planned, I waited for Kiddo to pull his shoes on and collect his book bag. He, however, was more interested in showing me bits of small paper. "I've made a card," he advised. "For the Leprechaun. Do you think he will come tonight?"

I silenced my inner groan along with several other choice words I won't print here. The next day was St. Patrick's Day, and I had nothing prepared. No Leprechaun traps. No pots waiting to be filled with gold. Nothing. When exactly had leprechauns coming to your house on St Patty's Day become a thing, anyway?

I could tell it was going to be a terrible, horrible, no good, very bad day.

When we got to the house, Kiddo made a bee-line to the television, ready to consume his daily allowance of cartoons. Her Royal Highness, our dog, made an equally determined path to the front door, ready to take care of her own daily requirements. I looked to Kiddo. I looked to Her Royal Highness. A walk would give me an opportunity to send a message to my mom regarding a certain

Leprechaun. "I'll be right back," I called. The cartoon's theme song was already playing as I closed the door.

Mom replied within short order, not for me to worry, however, Her Royal Highness had not yet done what we'd come out to let her do. Just then a cat appeared, and not just any cat—it was *the* cat. I couldn't tell you if that cat was the bravest animal I'd ever seen or stupidest. This is because, for whatever the reason, the cat was not only not afraid of dogs, it actively sought them out. It was not uncommon for this cat to follow us around the block during our walks. Sure enough, as soon as it spotted Her Royal Highness, it immediately crossed the road, causing a car to come full stop and angry looks shot my way.

Her Royal Highness passed her cat test before we brought her home. But still, I don't like to tempt fate, nor do I wish to be responsible for an injury of someone else's pet. Seeing no other choice, I led Her Royal Highness away. The cat followed. Only when we rounded a corner did the cat give up its pursuit. If I wasn't an animal lover who doesn't condone this line of thinking, I might hope you step on a tack, cat.

It was a terrible, horrible, no good, very bad day.

That's what it was because when we returned inside, the house was empty. Guess whose kid decided, in those short few minutes, that he missed me more than he wanted to watch his cartoons and had run off in the opposite direction with his brother while Her Royal Highness was being chased by a cat around the corner?

If what I'd felt during the workday was panic, the myriad of swirling emotions I experienced in that moment have yet to be named. I wondered if invisible fencing for children is allowed in Australia.

'I am having a terrible, horrible, no good, very bad day,' I texted my mom (or roughly something like that). I didn't look at my phone to see if she answered.

While I was scolding/hugging my children for giving me a fright, Mom showed up on my front porch with a frozen mix of Korean noodles in hand. It was a wonderful gesture, but they proved to be utterly inedible. Even Her Royal Highness turned it down.

Kiddo, wanting to show off for his Nana, took twice as long to do his homework than he usually does and LT, well LT was his normal self, but if I allowed LT access to the phone, he probably would have called Australia.

It was a terrible, horrible, no good, very bad day.

My husband didn't promptly return my texts, and I hate that.

Exhausted after the kids went to bed, I couldn't motivate myself to work on my work in progress and I hate a lost opportunity.

When I finally did hear from my children's father, it was clear he'd been having fun while I was not. I still hadn't figured out what to do about the Leprechaun outside of mom's vague assurances that all would be well and calling in sick to work the next day wasn't an option.

It had been a terrible, horrible, no good, very bad day.

My mom says some days are like that, even for people who might seem to have it all together.

I guess it's a good thing for me then, that my mom lives nearby and not in Australia.

Love you, Mom, and thanks.

The Invention

The eastern coast of the United States had been drenched for weeks. After days of constant precipitation, I had given up trying to limit the mess my housebound children left in their wake. However, when the sun finally emerged, I was quick to encourage my eldest son to go outside with his father while his brother napped so I might focus on interior damage control.

As I tidied up inside, I heard the distinctive whirl of a saw blade spinning in the garage. Kiddo must have come up with another building project for him and his father to work on, I thought while tuning the sound out of mind. A building project meant I would have at least another hour to myself. Sure enough, roughly an hour later, the door burst open and in walked Kiddo. He proudly held up a piece of scrap wood cut roughly a foot long. Tape attached a plastic spoon on one end with a plastic fork on the other.

"It's my invention," he bragged. "With this you don't have to lose time putting your fork down. You just spin it around and you have your spoon!"

His demonstration would have made the most seasoned infomercial marketers proud. I could almost hear him say, but wait, there's more . . . I tried not to laugh. I didn't have the heart to tell him that not only did someone else beat him to product launch, they've made it more efficient as well. Spork, anyone? Yeah, I've never heard of it either.

His brother woke, playtime (aka demolition derby) once again resumed, and the invention was forgotten. Eventually, though, it was dinnertime. As we set the table, Kiddo looked at the flatware next to his plate and then at me. "I don't need this stuff," he announced, returning the utensils to their drawer. "I've got my Spoonandfork! (TM, Patent Pending)" He looked at his brother. "Would you like one too?"

Yes, let's arm the three-year-old, who already spends far too much time playing with his food, with a pointy stick. What could possibly go wrong? "Honey, I really don't think he needs one of those . . ." I argued.

You could see the confusion in Kiddo's eyes. How could Mom not appreciate the life-changing potential of his invention? The disappointment, which transitioned almost immediately into understanding. She obviously just didn't get it.

Kiddo turned to his brother for support. His brother stared back. You could hear his thoughts as they formed. Yes, little brother wants the pointy stick. Give little brother the pointy stick. Kiddo's smile returned as he found a nearby marker and wrote his initial on the wood. "This one is mine, but I'll make you one, and when I do, I'll put your name on it."

My youngest stared at his brother in rapt adoration. Kiddo's grin returned and stretched from ear to ear. At least someone in this house gets it. As Kiddo returned to his spot at the table, I could tell as far as he was concerned, my informal product review was already forgotten and my argument, silenced. Flipping the pointy stick end over end, he eagerly dug into his meal. I am sure that first bite was delicious.

By the time we are adults, most of us have heard phrases like it's "already been done" or "that will never work," more times than we can count. We become jaded and stop inventing ways to make things better for ourselves. Instead, we rely on making do with whatever is already available, even if it means we have to settle for less than an ideal solution.

We stay at a job we hate because it pays the bills. We do the same routine day in and day out, even though it makes us feel as if we are drifting through life on auto-pilot, because there's security in stability. So fixated on reality, we turn our eyes away from possibility. In short, we give up without ever trying.

Mindfulness is an art, and one I highly recommend everyone practice. That being said, if you focus on the present as an adult, there's a good chance you will come to the conclusion being an adult isn't all that it's cracked up to be. This is why I say, practice mindfulness, but when you do try to do so from the perspective of a child.

Children who have yet to be jaded by the "it will never works," or "this is the best I can dos" can show us there's still magic in the everyday. There is wonder. There is possibility. There is still room for the what ifs and to imagine of something better. There's a lot we can learn by paying attention to the lessons children can teach us.

For example, I believe we all have a pointy stick buried somewhere deep in our minds—some problem-solving idea that could save us time, or more. And yet we've convinced ourselves the idea is ridiculous, a waste of money, or has been done before. To be honest, in most cases that little voice in the back of our head is probably right. However, the only way to know for sure is to consider an even more ridiculous possibility—it might just work.

No Signal

Twenty degrees. That's roughly the difference in temperature between my hometown and the mountains at the beginning of summer. Considering it was now reaching the nineties (or lower thirties if Celsius is more your thing), and the fact that our air-conditioning had decided to take some time off work in the summer of 2017, we decided a change of scenery was in order.

Tents and sleeping bags strapped to the car, we set out for the Pisgah National Forest, near Mount Mitchell, the highest point in the eastern United States. The park is part of the Appalachian Mountains, accessible through winding roads and the Blue Ridge Parkway. While you can, and I have, backpacked along the trail, there are also a number of more *civilized* camp sites scattered along the roadways offering bath houses and running water along with level ground for your tent. However, these operate on a strictly first come, first serve basis, which is why they recommend you call ahead.

We hadn't.

Knowing the risk that there might be no room at a particular site, we'd identified a location that might offer more than one option and plugged in the address into the navigation app on my husband's phone. While we drove, I scrolled down the webpage describing the area. Down at the bottom of the screen in bold text, the site read, 'As we are in a remote area, GPS directions may not be accurate. Click here for detailed directions.'

Our youngest, LT, demanded markers in the back where he was hard at work on his latest masterpiece. Our eldest, Kiddo, wanted a movie. My mom, who was brave enough to venture along with us, chatted about recent family news. I returned my phone to my bag, dismissing the site's warning. So what if we didn't find that exact site? There was sure to be another.

As the mountain roads twisted and turned, the back of the car grew silent. In Kiddo's case, this is a troubling sign as he is prone to motion sickness. We pulled over to give him some air. "Are we almost there?" he asked as we piled back into the car. We glanced at the navigation app. It read, 'No Signal'.

"Seven more miles to go," my husband replied. To me he added with a shrug, "at least, that's what it said before it dropped off." My mom offered her seat so that Kiddo could be closer to the open window.

Seven miles felt more like seventy. The signal never returned, and I grew increasingly chagrined for not looking at those step-by-step directions while I still had the chance. We could only assume we were still going in the right direction, as there was only one direction to go. Up. And Around. And Up some more.

We noticed the smell of campfires first. *Thank goodness*, I thought. The campsite wasn't the one we were originally targeting, but considering the shade of pale green on the faces of those in the back seats, it would have to do. Fortunately, a single site was still vacant.

Mom looked at her phone. "Still no signal," she replied.

Preferring to stream our music to downloading it, we were limited to listening to the same five to ten songs stored on the device on repeat as we pitched the tents (one for my mom and the boys the other for Her Royal Highness–our dog, my husband, and me), unpacked our supplies, and stoked the fire. As the sun began to set, we noticed dark clouds rolling in. "Do you think it is going to storm tonight?" My mom asked. I shrugged.

Storm—such a small word for such a big event in the wide-open.

Shortly after midnight, the wind picked up as lightning flashed across the sky, temporarily making the flimsy fabric of my tent appear as colorful as it appeared in bright day. Her Royal Highness sat at full attention in the center. Thunder boomed. Her Royal Highness whimpered. I sat up and tried to comfort her as the wind whipped at our sides. She nuzzled the flap that served as the door as if to say, let's go.

"Shh shh, it will be okay," I whispered as I felt along the flap's zipper and found a half-inch of water. At least, I hope so, I thought. A storm this intense couldn't go on for long. Or could it? My hands itched to locate my phone and bring up the radar, but once again—no signal. You don't realize how much you have grown to rely on constant connection until you are completely cut off.

The storm passed, though I didn't track it. We woke without alarms and ate when we were hungry. We found trails by looking at maps and by asking other humans for directions. The air remained cool and inviting as we ventured deeper into the forest until the only sign of people were the footprints left on paths made muddy and slick with rainwater and the occasional signpost or hand railing.

Before the day ended, we had walked roughly nine miles and seen stunning vistas and waterfalls made only more impressive from the storm. I'd watched my boys walk hand in hand as the trail became steep and attempted to memorize the moment as they called out "Brother Jump" before hopping off exposed roots together. It's a memory I fully plan to use to maximum embarrassment when they start dating.

That evening, which thankfully was thunderstorm-free, we ate the most amazing steak dinner, cooked over the fire ring's open flame as a neighboring site played music in a language we didn't recognize, but was music all the same. We laughed while Her Royal Highness snored. We chatted when normally we might scroll on our phones. We enjoyed being together. And before we called it a night, Kiddo told us it had been his favorite camping trip ever.

I may just agree.

We'd lost connectivity for a few days, it was true, but, as it turns out, we only strengthened our connection. All it had taken was a change of scenery and perhaps a difference of twenty degrees.

The Reading

I'd been booked for a reading, but not just any reading. No, this would not be some open mic style event at the nearby coffee shop, nor would I be reading to empty chairs at the local bookstore. I would be reading to a packed room, made up by the most discerning of audiences. An audience, I should add, who isn't afraid to tell you along with their friends and family exactly how you failed to live up to their expectations in excruciating detail.

I would be reading to my son's kindergarten class.

It was Dr. Seuss week at his elementary school and guest readers were invited to come in and share their love of reading with the next generation.

I arrived early armed with not one, but two books: *The Sneetches and Other Stories*, by Dr. Seuss himself, as well as *Dragon Was Terrible* by Kelly DiPucchio. They only expected me to read one story but felt the need to ensure I had a backup plan if the room turned on my selection.

I waited in the hall, eager to start, but hesitant to spoil the surprise (we hadn't told our son I would visit the class that day) or interrupt the lesson at hand. The school principal saw me in the hallway and smiled.

Then I was waved in and invited to sit in front of a group of smiling faces.

I made my choice. It was Dr. Seuss week, after all. I held up *The Sneetches* for all the children to see.

"I have that."

"I've heard it before."

"My dad reads that to me too."

Had I made the wrong choice? I wondered. *Guess, it's too late now.*

I opened the book to the story of The Zax which is a tale of two creatures called Zax—one north going, one south going—who meet one day in the prairie of Prax and once they meet neither Zax will budge from the direction of his tracks. And so, they stay stuck there, unbudging, for years while the rest of the world grows and leaves them behind.

The kids laughed at how silly both Zax had been, but they also pointed out the dangerous situation the Zax found themselves in. An overpass had been built around those stubborn Zax, and fast-moving cars now surrounded them. They couldn't have gotten to where either of them was going even if they tried. It was an aspect of the story I hadn't previously considered.

Afterward, I asked the children what the Zax should have done. Hands shot up.

"They should have gone around each other."

"One Zax should duck and roll forward so the other could jump over its top."

"One Zax could split in two so the other could go through the middle."

Admittedly, that last suggestion is a little more problematic than the other two, but I'd like to point out that at no time did a child suggest one Zax push the other out of the way, knock one to the ground to be stomped over, or otherwise use brute force to get where they were going. Instead, all they came up with were creative compromises.

I wound up reading the second book, *Dragon was Terrible*, as well. It was a story the majority of kids hadn't heard before.

A dragon who is terrible, of course, performs a series of, you guessed it, terrible acts around a kingdom (like taking candy away from a baby unicorn). The King announces he's had enough of the dragon's shenanigans and issues a challenge to his knights to do something about the beast. They aren't instructed to kill it, but tame it. Their attempts to beat the dragon into submission only make it more terrible. Then one day a small boy arrives, and he does something no one else in the kingdom has ever thought of—he gives the dragon a chance to be a hero.

Once again, I asked the kids at the end what the story had been about. Hands shot up. Although the story was new, they immediately understood its subtle theme about the power of inclusion.

Either this next generation is super smart or I'm starting to think more grown-ups should celebrate Dr. Seuss week too.

The Tale of the Improbable Boat

"ad!" Our eldest son called out one morning from the direction of the garage. "Dad!" He called again.

"What," his father yelled back from the den where we both sat still in our pajamas, nursing far too little coffee to match Kiddo's level of activity.

"We need your help," Kiddo called out. "For the boat project! Don't you remember?"

I glanced at my husband. "Boat project?" It was one of those times I had to debate with myself whether I really want to know.

Kiddo and one of his best friend's recently came across a waterfall only a few short yards from our backyard. I've lived in this house for years, but only learned of its existence when Kiddo returned one afternoon drenched from knee to toe. I can only assume that prior to their discovery it only existed in one of those secret magical places that only children are equipped to find.

Like any proud discoverers, both boys had immediately claimed the waterfall and the surrounding creek bed as their own. Now, it would seem, they had decided that it was time to take their exploration to the next level by building a boat.

My husband helped the boys pull down a few supplies, but left them to their work as Kiddo loves to work on his inventions. Occasionally, one would pop in to raid the pantry for a snack. As I cleaned up the kitchen, I heard the distinctive sound of a power screwdriver. Unable to contain my misgivings or curiosity any longer, I gave in and peeked at the work in progress. Their eyes lit up at my appearance. "Can you help?" the boys asked, holding out a piece of particle board and a pair of mismatched screws from the various piles now littered across the garage floor.

I eyeballed their creation. To my eye, its resemblance to a boat ended at—it's made of wood. "Um, I am not sure how well that will float." I mean, it wasn't impossible to think it might keep water out by the time they were done, but it appeared highly improbable.

"That's why we need your help to attach the sides," Kiddo's friend replied, showing me just how the pieces of mismatched wood were supposed to fit together.

Oh, is that all you need?

I left shortly afterward, no more confident in their boat's design than I was minutes earlier. I saw a flash of color run past a window. Perhaps, I thought the boys had given up or grown bored and gone to play another game. I saw another flash. Both kids reappeared in the garage, their arms now full of bright yellow pull ties and something I could only guess was the rubber shell of a bicycle tire 'borrowed' from the other house. Or perhaps not.

By the end of the morning, their creation was no more boat-shaped than it was when they started (it looked more like a ramp), but it was theirs. Undeterred and full of smiles, the pair picked it up and took off toward the woods and the newest adventure, but within minutes they were once again in the garage.

"Didn't work out like you thought?" I said, my heart full of sympathy. "That's okay, at least you gave it a try."

"Yeah," Kiddo said with a grin. "We just need to build a dock."

I found the boys in the woods later that day with another board, their 'dock,' laying on one side of the creek bed and their 'boat' drifting downstream, just out of arm's reach. Obviously, their grand plan to set sail across the seven seas to continents unknown hadn't exactly worked out as they'd expected, but just as clearly it hadn't stopped them from having an adventure all the same.

And rather than focusing on the loss of one morning's effort, they were already planning their next foray.

I am trying to be more like my children. It is the reason I tell these stories. It is the reason I keep coming back to these writings week after week, even when I sometimes feel like quitting. I remind myself, I wouldn't have known the creek existed had the children not risked exploring. I wouldn't have thought there was a need for a boat, let alone a dock, as the water was only knee deep on a child. But these children of mine, they never seem bothered by the reasons I might come up off the top of my head why not to do something or why something won't work. They simply try and enjoy the experience.

Not everything is going to go to plan. Not every idea will float. I have to remind myself that is okay. Because while I may lose a few screws along the way, in the end, I know, regardless of the results, the mere attempt can often prove to be an adventure worth having.

The Place Where the Sidewalk Ends

*L*T sat on the tire swing in our backyard, alone. His brother had gone to play with a friend, leaving LT to amuse himself while his father and I completed our chores. His legs were curled up as they wouldn't touch the ground even if extended. As a result, the swing was nearly motionless except for a gentle sway with the breeze. I watched as his mouth move and wondered what conversation he was having with himself might be about. He looked content, but it was a lonely image.

The last of my cleaning could wait. "Do you want to go to the park?" I called out, thinking there might be other kids he could play with. LT beamed, eagerly accepting my offer, and soon we were walking down the street to our local playground. LT chattered about things like clouds, giants, and other friendly monsters, smiling at everybody we passed along the way. Never once did I have to tell him to hurry, or stay with me, or explain why he shouldn't be carried. *Who was this child?*

At the park, the sun shone down with only a few clouds breaking up the brilliant expanse of the otherwise blue sky. I settled onto a bench inside the playground as LT climbed up on the play set designed for the bigger kids. "Look at me," he shouted as he crawled through the plastic tunnel connecting a pair of slides.

I wondered why on earth we were the only ones at the park on such a lovely day? LT slid down the larger of the slides. "It's too hot mommy," he advised as he reached the bottom. I realized the kid wasn't exaggerating as I touched the plastic. The equipment could serve as a skillet if it was any hotter. I now understood why the playground was empty.

LT's brother wouldn't return for another hour or so. "How about we go on a waterfall hunt," I suggested. The greenway, a series of hidden wooded paths that weave in and out of my city, was not too far away. We just had to go to the end of the sidewalk. LT beat me to the gate.

The temperature dropped a good five to ten degrees Fahrenheit as we made our way down the gravel path connecting the trail with the outside world. As always, I felt as if we'd been teleported to some distant place as the canopy of trees stretched out above us. "This way," LT requested, pointing toward one of his favorite places along the path—a small bridge arching over an even smaller stream.

Leaving the trail, we descended to the stream below. Large rocks enabled LT to step halfway across where he dipped his fingers into the water at the top of the small falls. "Can a waterfall move?" he asked.

"I suppose it can," I answered, "but it takes some time to move on its own."

We ventured further along the stream bed to where the bank was broken up by a myriad of smaller rocks and pebbles. LT reached down and grabbed a handful of dirt. Throwing it into the water, we watched as it dispersed into a ribbon-like cloud as the current took it downstream. LT grabbed a larger rock. This one too fell into the water with a plunk, but unlike the dirt, the rock remained in place. You could almost see the gears turning in his head.

"Can you make a waterfall?" he asked.

Once again, I nodded, and soon he was grabbing rocks, twigs, and bits of dirt. The water bulged where LT had added his obstacles, rising over the additional rocks as it rejoined the existing flow. It was hardly Niagara Falls, but it was enough of a difference in height for LT to declare success.

I knew by this time his brother was likely home and would look to share his own adventures with us. "Are you ready to go home and tell Daddy all about your waterfall?" I asked.

"But it's not my waterfall, mommy," he answered with a smile. "It's ours."

"All I did was stand here," I countered as my heart did a little flip-flop as it tried not to melt.

"But you were here with me," he replied.

It was a comment that probably kept him from getting grounded for life when he decided to lock himself in his room later that night in protest rather than get ready for bed.

I've thought about the stream and our waterfall. He only moved a few rocks, true, but even so, the stream will never be exactly the same. The newly formed eddy, as small as it is, will cut into the stream bed, creating fresh paths for the current to flow. These underwater paths, these series of slight adjustments, might go for years unseen but will continue to trigger more changes. Another rock might shift. Another eddy will form. Until one day, years from now, someone might dip his or her finger into the top of a waterfall where one did not previously exist—all thanks to LT and the difference he made.

It will be our waterfall too, because we're never as alone as it seems. It will also serve as proof we can, in fact, move waterfalls if we are first willing to make a small change.

Persistence

A few years ago, my mom gave my eldest son a pair of training roller skates. My son is a fan of instant gratification. When he put the skates on and immediately lost his footing, he grew frustrated and lost interest in learning the new skill. I placed the skates on a shelf in our garage.

After some time passed. I would see the skates and ask him if he would be willing to try it again. To give my son credit, he would go along with my suggestion, but then would fall down and rapidly lose interest once again. Finally, one day he seemed to get the hang of the process. Sort of. He was able to stay up on his feet, but instead of rolling from point "a" to point "b," he would pick up his foot and walk there. It rather defeated the purpose and was a little frustrating to watch.

My husband and I had the brilliant idea that I should strap on my own skates and show him how it was done. The house I had grown up in had been on a cul-de-sac, a round, closed no-through road, which didn't see a ton of traffic. This gave the neighborhood kids a perfect place to go for any number of outdoor games and activities. At times, it was like our own personal skating rink. I might not have been good enough to compete in something like roller derby, but I was pretty confident on wheels throughout my childhood and teenage years. I ran to pull my skates out of our closet.

As I strapped my feet into my roller blades, it occurred to me that I hadn't dusted off my skates in several years. My legs wobbled as I stood up. How in the world did I used to do this? The slight incline of my driveway was suddenly extremely intimidating. I heard my husband tell our son, "now look how mommy does it." Can you say performance anxiety? All I needed was to fall down and crack my head open. We'd never get kiddo to try something new ever again.

I made it down the driveway through a combination of slaloming and walking on the grass. Graceful, I was not. I had wanted to teach my son my skate moves. Instead I taught him that grown-ups need practice sometimes too, even on skills we think we have long since mastered.

I do not write about topics like positive thinking because I am a Pollyanna—an eternal optimist. I do not see rainbows with every rainstorm. I succumb to pessimism now and then just like everyone else. But I have chosen to record uplifting thoughts because this is how I practice my own internal motivation.

I am reminded of the advice: do not practice until you get it right, practice until you can't get it wrong. Self-motivation is one skill I may never master, and I am okay with that, but every day is an opportunity to practice.

Changing Parameters

I love food, and my husband can do some wonderful things in the kitchen, but mealtimes are one of the most stressful times of the day for me. All because my toddler has strong opinions what he does, and does not, want to eat.

My eldest son hadn't always been willing to eat his food either. Beginning from the time he was his brother's age, each time he ate everything on his plate, we broke out into a little song about being a member of the clean plate club as a way of encouragement. It was a tradition we continued as he grew older. It also helped that we gave those earning membership into the exclusive clean plate club privileges, such as dessert or extra TV time.

It was once again dinner time, and I could tell it was going to be another one of those nights. After several minutes, my son's dinner was just as untouched as it had been when it was set down. Until suddenly it wasn't.

Within a blink, the entire contents of the plate had been shuffled neatly from plate to place-mat, thereby conforming to our other rule: no throwing food. He beamed at both my husband, announcing with a smile, "Keen Pate Cub!"

I have to admit he was technically correct. The plate was clean.

If he was older, someone might accuse my toddler of being a cheat. But that wouldn't be accurate. Silly us. We hadn't specifically said the food had to have been eaten, only that the plate be clean. In the words of Captain Kirk, he didn't cheat. He merely changed the parameters, providing us with the outcome he thought we wanted without unnecessary (his opinion) sacrifice.

My poor youngest son is destined for entrepreneurship. He just doesn't know it yet.

There are a number of websites out there that describe the traits necessary to be a successful entrepreneur. If you were you to run a search, you would find terms like tenacity, resiliency, perseverance, and risk taking.

As the wife of an entrepreneur, I fully agree that these are necessary traits and skills that will definitely come in handy. But these are traits that are most useful only after the business has been launched. To get to that point, you must first be able to visualize how to get what you want in a new and innovative way.

You have to be willing to accept that nothing is impossible. We just haven't figured out a way to achieve it yet.

Resolutions

We usually watch the Rose Parade at my house during our New Years celebrations. It is an event which, under non-pandemic conditions, takes place in Pasadena, California, each year. Similar to Macy's Thanksgiving Day Parade in terms of network coverage and national tradition, the parade features marching bands and the occasional musical act, but unlike its northeastern relation, this parade relies on drivable "floats" decorated using only botanicals rather than on the same reusable balloons.

As I watch the parade coverage, I am constantly amazed by the amount of detailing that goes into each of these floats. Groups spend a year or more designing these displays, planning the look to the last petal. There might be a dragon that can bat its eye or a giant bicyclist who can tip his hat. You never know what you are going to see until it makes its way down the boulevard. Which is why I've gotten frustrated over the years with the trend in network coverage to skip floats in order to have more time to promote their Spring line-up or break for the millionth commercial.

This is why in 2018, I decided to mix up my annual viewing tradition by doing something different. I watched the Funny or Die / Amazon Prime's coverage of the event hosted by Will Ferrell and Molly Shannon under the guise of their fake personalities, Cord Hosenbeck, and Tish Cattigan instead of listening to the same mix of daytime news crew-members and B-list celebrities.

The coverage was a satire, though the joke was on hosts like themselves rather than parade participants, and what made me chuckle the most was a bit the pair did on New Year's Resolutions.

At the beginning of the parade, they talked about the resolutions they'd set for themselves for 2017. Tish's, for example, was to "put herself out there and let the universe be her guide." They talked about their relative success. Tish's felt she'd really taken that risk and grown as a person by attending a wine class. Then, at the end, they announced their resolutions for 2018.

They were EXACTLY the same, delivered in a blissfully unaware deadpan voice.

Were Amazon to bring these characters back in the next year, or the year after that, I expected this would become a recurring bit. They would discuss the same resolutions and the same results year after year. We can imagine it because when it comes to New Year's resolutions, that's the sort of thing so many of us in real life do too.

We resolve to lose the same 15 pounds or eat less of the same junk. We resolve to spend more time on our personal interests or travel more as if by the stroke of midnight on Jan 1st, we can suddenly invent more hours in the day or money in the bank. We tell ourselves it didn't work last year, but it would this time because this year was different—we were different.

It's not entirely a lie either. We ARE different. However, the difference usually comes down to one thing—we are older. The rest is pretty much the same. Thus, ensuring that the next time the end of the year comes around we will find ourselves in the exact same place we are at its beginning.

Which brings me to my point. In order to truly be anything other than simply an older version of ourselves, we have to be willing to make a significant change at least once in our lifetimes.

I'm not talking about a change in hairstyle or taking a new route to the job. Something significant. Something that challenges what you've done before and what you think you know. Something that involves a risk and is guaranteed to make an impact.

Whether that impact will prove to be good or bad, only time will tell, but one thing is certain—you will not just be older after trying, you'll be wiser too.

Contemplating Success at the Corner Bus Stop

*P*ublic school bus routes vary in my area almost as much as the weather, but for a few years my eldest, and later his brother, rode the same bus a pair of their cousins did. This happenstance was great from the kids' perspective. However, it was even better for us adults and our bosses, as it gave us the opportunity to rotate who'd stay with them at the stop so that the rest could get to work on time.

It was my morning. My morning to supervise them at home following drop-off as they pulled out every toy I had so painstakingly put away just days before. My morning to ensure they reached the bus stop with backpacks and lunch sacks intact.

Some mornings those tasks are easier than others.

I informed the crew it was time to clean up. My youngest, LT, pouted. "Now, honey," I started. He pouted some more. "Five-year-olds are big enough to pick up their own mess." He grumbled and whined, but it satisfied me to see the toy go back into its spot.

My youngest wouldn't join the rest on the big yellow bus until the following year. This meant that on my morning, I would drop him off with the wonderful woman who watched him during the day while I worked before taking the rest of my charges to their destination. But this morning, one of the kids asked if LT might come to the bus stop with them instead. Another chimed in — they wanted to race. I looked at the clock. We'd have to wait outside longer than normal, were they sure?

Spring had come early to my neck of the woods that year. We'd spent the last two weekends with the kids outside and the windows open. Already the trees and flowers were budding and small pink petals dotted the streets. My concern about a few minutes' extra exposure to the great outdoors fell on deaf ears.

Fine, I'd thought. I'd be democratic about it — this time.

I altered our course, and soon we were at the stop. The children dumped their bags at the corner by my feet and congregated a few yards away — close enough for me to keep an eye on them, but far enough that they might whisper among themselves unheard. The next thing I knew, they were running down the sidewalk back toward me.

Or more specifically, LT ran. Kiddo, my eldest, and my nephew, on the other hand, took turns moving in what I can only describe as spastic hop, yet tiny tip-toe sized step that would have only impressed a snail with progress. As a result, LT passed them with ease. My youngest then ran around me, grinning from ear to ear. When LT returned to their starting point/finish line, both his brother and my nephew tried to one-up each other in exaggerated groans about how fast their youngest competitor now was. It was a far cry from the fits and tantrums we used to experience about 'unfair' contests and proof of how mature the boys had become.

Before long other children arrived, filling up the sidewalk and preventing further races. One child shouted "Bus," like a whaler of old spotting a blowhole out at sea as the big yellow vehicle appeared from around the corner. The kids scrambled to pick up their backpacks and gathered in a line as LT returned to my side.

Picking him up, we waved at the faces grinning at us from the other side of the windows. "That's going to be you soon," I told my youngest as the bus pulled away. "Are you ready?"

He smiled and nodded, undoubtedly thinking that the coming school year would be filled with fun and games like the time he'd just had.

Recalling the display at being asked to put toys away, I made this a teachable moment. "You know, when you are in school, you are going to have to listen to your teacher when he or she tells you to do things."

LT looked at me and cocked his head to one side. "Why?"

"Because you don't want to go to the principal's office or get bad grades."

The look of confusion on LT's face only deepened. He repeated, "Why?"

"Because they will call mommy or give mommy a bad report. You don't want that."

He chewed on my answer for a moment or two. "Okay mommy, I'll listen to my teacher." I smiled and patted his head. Then softly, I almost missed it, LT muttered, "sometimes."

LT might have thought he was ready for school, but I had to wonder if his school would be ready for him.

Later, our conversation made me think of my own plans for the future and some of the stumbling blocks I've already encountered. Often, I complain about how long these plans are taking as patience is not my best virtue.

The morning then became a good reminder that while I might achieve the measures by which I currently judge my success, there will always be challenges I have yet to envision.

Therefore, I cannot, will not let those unforeseen bumps discourage me completely. I have to remind myself of those that traveled a similar path before me, of those who didn't know then what they know now, and how they matured along the way. Every day, as I take another step down that path, I tell myself, I am closer now than ever before, even if I am forced to retrace a few steps or take the occasional detour.

Because that is what I do. That is what I've done.

Though it sometimes seems I still have a long way yet to go, I know that when (not if) I finally reach the future of my dreams, the bigger question is now: will my dreams be ready for me?

A Bump in the Night

Bump. Muffle. Jingle. Thump.

My eyes snapped open. The room was dark, except for the clock's display, which showed it was only a few minutes past three in the morning.

Bump. Muffle. Jingle. Thump.

My heart raced. However, my husband's rhythmic breathing to my side was a clear indicator that the sound from the downstairs hadn't yet penetrated through his dreams as it had mine. Darn my sensitive 'mom' ears.

Bump. Muffle. Jingle. Thump.

I sat up as I tried to imagine what could be causing the sound. We'd had unseasonably warm weather recently, enjoying a weekend of open doors and windows. Could an animal have gotten inside? It wouldn't be the first time. Several years ago we'd awoken to another strange scratching sound. That time, the sound had woken us both up as it came from directly outside of our bedroom door. I can still my husband's gasp of "it's a cat," when he opened the door. As it turned out, our neighbors were watching a friend's cat, which had gotten out at some point during the night.

Disoriented, or simply curious, it had pushed through the flap of the dog door we'd neglected to close all the way and explore our home. Lucky for it, our dog, Sir Ruff, was tucked away inside his own room. He was not a fan of intruders in his territory and would run around barking all night at imagined threats or offending shadows if given run of the house. He was also very good at catching smaller animals, which was something we found out years before. Had he been on patrol that night, I could imagine all too easily the uncomfortable conversation we would have to have with the neighbors in the morning.

But, I reminded myself with no small hurt, Sir Ruff had crossed the rainbow bridge some four years earlier. We also kept the pet doors permanently sealed now. Sir Ruff's successor, Her Royal Highness, refused to use them. She had servants to open doors. It would be an affront to her royal pride to open a door on her own.

Bump. Muffle. Jingle. Thump.

My imagination expanded in the darkness. While the sound was quiet enough to be caused by an animal, it seemed unnaturally controlled and repetitive to be produced by something wild, but still not out of the realm of possibilities. I turned to my sleeping husband. Someone was going to have to risk the unknown. Someone had to go investigate. Someone needed to wake up.

Bump. Muffle. Jingle. Thump.

It seemed my preferred someone had developed an immunity to my glares over our years of marriage. I debated shaking him awake. Reminding myself that I am a strong woman capable of fighting my own battles (or at least screaming loud enough to alert the neighbors), I decided against it. It wasn't as if I was going back to sleep without knowing the cause of the sound. While telling myself the sound could be a mouse or Her Royal Highness herself—though that would mean she'd left the comfort of her pillows. I supposed it could even be one of our children—I'd caught Kiddo sleepwalking once before. Resigned to investigate, I left the bed and slowly opened the bedroom door.

Bump. Muffle. Jingle. Thump.

Swallowing my fear, I crept toward the staircase and peered over the banister.

Bump. Muffle. Jingle. Thump.

Movement caught my eye.

Bump. Muffle. Thump.

The sound was coming from . . . I squinted in the darkness . . .

Bump. Muffle. Thump.

An array of blue LEDs appeared in the darkness. They belonged to the robotic sweeper vacuum I'd received for Christmas, which I'd forgotten we'd programmed to clean while we slept. The white disk-shaped robot attempted to maneuver its way out from under our dining room table. Bump. Hitting one of the chair legs, it rotated a fraction of an inch and tried again.

Bump. Whirl.

The robot turned once more, disappearing once again under the table, only to return a moment later for another attempt at escape.

Adrenaline fled my system, as my body reminded me exactly how early it was. Now that I understood where the sound was coming from, there was no more reason to fear. Instead, it became no more than white noise and something I could ignore. I returned to bed as the robot continued its chore.

It seems we are being bombarded by new things to fear. Things to lose sleep over. I am reminded often of the words of Franklin Roosevelt who said during his first inaugural address, "The only thing we have to fear is fear itself."

But there is even more to the speech than this one memorable quote. He called this fear of fear a "nameless, unreasoning, unjustified terror which paralyzes needed efforts to convert retreat into advance."

He called upon the people to recognize that it was fear, above all, that was the nation's enemy and introduced the policy of the good neighbor: "the neighbor who resolutely respects himself and, because he does so, respects the rights of others."

History has a way of repeating itself and I find the words of this speech as true now as they were during the time they were first spoken. It is only the size of the stage that has changed.

We are in danger of losing our ability to respect the views of others—those that live differently, speak differently, pray differently or in cases, vote differently and in doing so jeopardize respect for ourselves. We are in danger of losing the battle with fear. And so, I implore you, no matter where you call home, or side of an issue's spectrum you take, to never lay awake in fear at the sound of a bump in the night. Instead, get out of your comfort zone. Investigate its source so you might better understand it from all angles.

That bump in the night may prove to be something terrible—something to be fought, but it might just as easily be something or someone trying to help you as best they can. You'll only know for sure how best to react if you first break the paralysis of fear, step forward and risk a look.

When Life Is Determined to Get In Your Way

My eldest son became sick. No, it wasn't COVID. That joy hadn't yet made its debut, but it wasn't a little cold either. He'd caught a strain of the flu that had been featured on every newscasts before the larger stories took over the airways. However, I didn't need to hear a bunch of statistics like how many other children were taking ill, or how dangerous the virus could be. I knew, even without watching a leading story on the television, how important it was to care for him and that monitoring his symptoms was an absolute must.

If that hadn't been enough, the forecast called for snow. Again. It was in the seventies (twenty-two Celsius). the week before, but I live in North Carolina. We can go through an entire year's worth of seasons in a week. In fact, we add a few more to the list, there's also pollen season and hurricane season too. (Yes, yes, Colorado—where you can have all four seasons in a single hour—I know we have nothing on you).

But normally it doesn't snow more than once or twice a year in the South, which is exactly why my parents moved us here when I was a kid. As a result, most of the people who live around here don't have a clue what to do when the white stuff falls other than to rush out and get milk and bread like it will become the new world currency.

I had just gotten my eldest dosed with fever reducer and settled under blankets when I received word that the school system would release my other son three hours early. Snow hadn't even started falling, but classes for the rest of the day were canceled. I needed to make sure I was there to meet his bus.

I received another alert. Not only had the school closed early, the following morning's opening would be delayed by three hours. My youngest was only in kindergarten at the time. He didn't yet understand the concept of social distancing and wanted nothing more than to spend time with his brother. Keeping him from breathing the same air as his older sibling would be a challenge all by itself.

My eldest's fever climbed to one hundred two point six.

The family calendar showed my hubby would be out of town for the balance of the week.

And then beta feedback for my most recent WIP came back as a solid 'meh,' signifying major re-writes were required.

There were doctors' appointments to make, prescriptions to fill, dinners to cook, and Her Royal Highness to walk, not to mention the work needed to be made up from the day we'd already missed between school and the day job. While juggling all of this, I needed to re-write thousands of words per day if I had any hope of reaching my writing-related goals.

And yet, during my regular writing time, when most of the house is either quiet or asleep, I found myself staring at a closed black laptop. I didn't even have the energy to lift the lid, let alone turn the machine on. I felt I'd broken something. My creative muscle simply refused to work.

Which brings me to the topic at hand, how do you remain focused on your goals when life is determined to get in your way? You start by giving yourself permission to let something go.

With the exception of the week between Christmas and New Year, I'd been posting something on my blog weekly for a few years. My blog posts, on average, are between 500 and 1200 words, meaning I've published more than the three books attributed to my name on my Amazon author page at this point. I taken pride in my consistency. I viewed it as keeping my promise to my readers, but something had to give.

As much as I loved my blog for the outlet it provided and the community it built, my number one goal wasn't to be a world-renowned as a blogger. Scaling back my efforts for a week, under the circumstances, was an easy choice to make (as was giving up on cleaning my house for a few days).

This is why you should never confuse artificial targets with your real goals.

What do you mean? Aren't they the same thing? No. A goal is where you want your arrow to go. The target around the goal just helps you aim. Hitting the target alone isn't enough. It's the bulls-eye you want.

For example, my target in 2018 was to release the sequel to *An Uncertain Faith* in May. That target, however, was really nothing more than a release schedule, a deadline to help keep me motivated day in and day out. My goal, on the other hand, was to write a book that lives up to, if not exceeds, the reader's expectations. Quality, therefore, was my goal, and frankly, there was no way I could achieve that goal unless I was willing to re-position my metaphorical bow and aim at a target more reflective of my current environment.

The next step anyone struggling with the average run-of-the-mill type of daily overwhelm is to ignore the urge to splurge. Once you have agreed to let certain lesser priorities go and/or readjusted your timeline after a period of stress or frantic activity, you may find yourself with feeling like there is this hole you have to fill. I've been told others call this strange sensation, 'having spare time.' Unaccustomed to spare time you will be tempted to take on additional tasks or responsibilities which sound easy in theory but are not in line with either your priorities or your goals. This is a trap.

Life will fill in that time for you just fine on its own. Trust me.

Third, you have to accept that setbacks happen to everyone. Even to people who appear to have it all together in public.

Next—and this can often be one of the more difficult steps to master—don't equate giving yourself a break with giving up. They aren't the same thing. We go to sleep with every expectation of waking up and doing it all over again in the morning. This is because a body needs rest to do its best. You need to adopt the same mindset for your goals.

I would still finish writing my book. It just didn't hit the bookshelves until after summer, instead of in the early spring. I didn't give up. I was able to pick the work back up after my break because I understood that a setback does not signify the end. I took my break, but then when life returned to more of a manageable routine, I got back in my chair, plotting forward once more. It also proved to be good training for maintaining my creative spark during lockdown, but that is another story.

Because the most important step is this last one. When life is determined to get in the way of your goals, the best thing you can do is to never stop trying.

Impostor Syndrome and the Fear of Success

*A*s much as I would like to deny that more than a decade has passed since I walked the halls of a high school as a student, I was expected to attend my husband's reunion as his plus one. The event took place in October, but its proximity to Halloween wasn't the reason I was scared, especially as the days leading up to the event drew shorter.

My husband told me not to worry, but that was easy for him to say. It was much more difficult for me to do. This is because He and I are polar opposites when it comes to networking events. He lights up as he mingles in the center of the room with anyone and everyone. He memorizes names, occupations, next of kin, and random off-hand personal statements which prove he was actively listening (it is a talent he doesn't always demonstrate at home with me, mind you, but no one is perfect). I dare say he lives for events like these.

I, on the other hand, prefer to lurk closer to the perimeter or spend the entire event with one particular person or group. The only thing I memorize with ease is the location of the exits. I hide, nibbling on finger foods or sipping on coffee or wine—anything that can give me an excuse not to talk to people I don't know while working up the courage to do just that. It's one of the joys of being an introvert at heart.

The funny thing is, while I am an introvert, I enjoy meeting people. I enjoy hearing their stories. I enjoy sharing mine. What I don't like, though, is the fear that takes over my brain and settles into my bones and causes me to slur my words or stutter and gesture with my hands like a madwoman when surrounded by strangers at an event promoting myself rather than say, a product or company. It is the fear of saying something wrong and being deemed a fraud or an impostor.

So when I say I was nervous about going to my husband's reunion, it was because personal experience had told me I had every reason to be. The entire room might be filled with people my husband had known since kindergarten. I knew these people were going to be more interested in learning about the person my husband had grown to be than in the person he'd married. However, I also knew that there would be at least one person waiting to trip me up. This person was me as I am my own worst enemy.

All it would take is for a single person to ask the small talk staple, "What is it you do?"

This question keeps me up the night before I attend any event with a large group of strangers. It is because my answer is complicated. I have a lot of interests. However, for every accomplishment I might rattle off, a disclaimer lays equally ready to roll off my tongue.

I manage a team, but that's not my passion.

I write books and publish articles, but I'm not currently in airports kiosks or other brick and mortar stores.

I create logos, book covers, and graphic designs, but it's just an extra service I offer. It doesn't pay the bills.

I am aware of the danger of this language and all the reasons I should use it, yet I can't seem to stop peppering words like only, not, and just, throughout my reply. I suppose you can say I like big BUTs and I cannot lie.

At times, this diversity of occupation has made me feel like a jack of all trades. That said, under certain conditions, like being asked what I do, it has also made me feel like a master of none. However, the worst part about this feeling is the knowledge I'm most likely judging myself harsher than anyone else is. Ah, Impostor Syndrome, I know thee well.

But at least, in those moments of doubt, I know I am not alone. According to a psychological study on the subject, seventy percent of people suffer from feelings that their good isn't and may never be good enough.

Impostor Syndrome or Imposter, if you prefer the alternate spelling, is a term coined by researchers Pauline R. Clance and Suzanne A. Imes back in 1978. It's used to describe someone who remains stubbornly convinced that their accomplishments were based on good fortune, lucky timing, or the having the right sympathetic friends, rather than their own merit. While the original study was fixated on women, an excessive amount of testosterone is no surefire protection against the plague of self-doubt.

People suffering from this syndrome display symptoms such as a tendency to discount their success and to over-work to a fault. They also can't help comparing their struggles to others and finding their efforts to be lacking.

So what then are the secrets for coping? I say coping because I'm not here to tell you how to overcome feeling like an impostor. I have yet to master that particular mind trick, but there are ways to work through the feelings of self-doubt when they arise. The first is to recognize the numbers are in your favor.

I'll repeat it again, seventy percent of people, worry that their efforts will never be good enough. In addition, if you only were to ask those considered who were considered successful by their peers, fifty percent would admit to feelings of inadequacy. So if I described you when I rattled off the symptoms, you're in good company. This means the people you meet at a party, networking event, or even smaller setting, are more likely to be concerned about protecting themselves then about calling you out.

The next strategy is to focus on positive. If you believe there is still an opportunity to grow or improve, then as long as you stay with it, that's exactly what you'll do. Therefore, embrace your inexperience, it makes you that much more a relatable and interesting a person.

I also save notes of thanks, praise, or random compliments given over the years to refer back to on days I don't feel so shiny.

It's maintaining perspective.

After all that worry, I was only asked once about myself.

Admittedly, this might have had something to do with the fact I'd spent much of the evening chatting with a single couple rather than mingling about the room. It also didn't hurt I'd known this couple since college. It just so happened, they'd also attended my husband's high school. But still. After so much preparation and nervous anticipation, it felt a wee bit anticlimactic, disappointing even, not to have been asked to launch into an over the top justification of all my life's decisions at least twice.

This is not to say I was disappointed in the event. The venue was lovely. The handful of people I managed to meet were great, though our conversation typically consisted of: "so where are you living now?", "how many kids do you have?", and "did you see which way your husband went?" It seems they were just more interested in catching up with their long-absent classmates than learning all about some stranger he brought in from the street. It was enough to make you think that was the entire point of a reunion. Go figure.

So, I didn't dazzle, nor did I amaze, but I had a good time, which I think counts for something. The question is, does it count enough?

When researching Impostor Syndrome, I came across another social fear, one even more destructive: achievemephobia—the Jonah Complex—also known as the fear of success.

At the time, I skimmed over it. I brushed it off. I didn't fear success. I've told myself that I view success as something different from giant houses or fast cars. It is freedom, security, and time with the family. It's not fame or fortune (though I'd somehow find it in myself to accept either). It's not something to be feared.

But then, like the glutton for punishment for research, I am, I clicked on links. I read further.

What if success is only temporary? How will I handle success being taken away? After working so hard to get this far, would I really be willing to do it all again?

What if my success makes me a target? What if it endangers those I love? Do I really to risk that kind of attention?

What if success changes me? What if it changes my relationships with others?

What if the world finds out I don't have what it takes? (Impostor Syndrome rearing its head)

What if my success means I no longer have time to spend with the people I care about or doing the other things I love?

What if I like routine? Why should I risk disrupting it?

People with this fear aren't typically lazy but they make excuses like "I don't have the time right now," or "I'll get it done after I take care of xyz." They procrastinate, while to everyone else it looks like they are busy achieving. They redirect. They go out of their way to ensure the goal line remains right where it is, in sight, but just out of reach. This way they never have to truly deal with their fear of the what ifs or learn the answers to these questions. Their fear of larger success is a killer and makes their failure a certainty.

I don't blame them. Seeing these questions in black and white, the lack of certain answers scare me too.

I had a good time at the reunion, but after so much preparation, I now feel as if I could have done more. I am wondering if there might be a little more fear of success in me than I'd like to admit, but the past is past. All I can do now is to be aware and try harder the next time.

Fear can actually be a good thing in our lives. A healthy fear of pain keeps us from sticking our hand on a hot burner. Fear of heights keeps us from dancing on a cliff's edge. A fear of sharks can make for entertaining stories and awesome blog fodder. We all have them.

You fear the burner because you've been burned.

You fear the edge because you've fallen

You fear sharks because . . . well, that's just good sense.

You fear success because because the unknown is stubbornly uncertain and terrifying in its possibility.

The difference between a fear of success and other phobias is its focus on what could happen in the future rather than what has happened in the past, but that doesn't mean it is a fear any less able to be managed or overcome.

Just as we wouldn't recognize the good in our lives if we didn't experience the bad, understanding our fears and finding the way to rise above them is what separates the brave from the idiotic. Fear can be a teaching mechanism too. So, I am not afraid to admit I have fears, but I am learning to ask better questions, like how I can stop poisoning my goals, and how I can stop standing in the way of my own success.

Jeopardy

*T*here is a long running trivia game show here in the U.S. that goes by the name of Jeopardy. Perhaps you have heard about it?

Growing up, it was understood in my house that when it was on you were paying attention and trying to answer the questions before the contestants (or anyone else in the family room) or you were outside. We were allowed to shout, but we had to at least try to answer the questions. Those watching would not accept any interruption.

I found my way outside more than a few times (Wheel of Fortune was more my game), however my older sister took this time and the house rules seriously. Her ability to absorb useless trivia puts my kids' old diapers to shame. It didn't surprise me at all then when I learned she had earned the right to be an actual contestant on the show, and not the watered-down teen or celebrity edition either, I mean the real version.

She got off to a slow start (malfunctioning buzzer was partly to blame), but then dominated a whole category. Even the host sounded a little stunned by her performance. (Seriously, how many people know the full breed names of dogs owned by European royalty outside of breeders, the American Kennel Club, or international equivalent? More importantly, *why* do these people know that?). She was securely in second place in the last round with the possibility of taking the win. The music ended, and her final answer was shown. She nailed it! Then they revealed her wager. It hadn't been enough for her to take over the top position. She remained in second place. Her run on the game show was over.

We knew how well she fared before the show aired, but still we watched the broadcast, hoping for a different outcome. She explained her strategy for her wager in the final round. She had gone into the game determined not to finish third and had wagered accordingly. As a result, second place was good enough and second place was what she achieved.

I am extremely proud of my sister. She was brave enough to go on national television and show off exactly how nerdy she could be. She achieved one of her childhood dreams and she was good at it—but she could have been great. She fell into the trap of thinking that in order to succeed, failure couldn't be an option, and as a result she played it safe rather than playing to win.

This happened several years ago. She and I had barely started our respective careers. Neither of us, at the time, were considering pursuing anything remotely entrepreneurial. We were both much more risk adverse back then. We both preferred to play things safe and to pursue the surefire. The lesson stuck with me anyway.

It made me realize third place isn't that bad as long as you gave it your all, and it doesn't mean you can't try again (real life is more forgiving than a game show in that regard). The risk of failure is always there, whether you accept it is an option. You can play it safe, and it can still find you. My sister taught me that sometimes if you want to be the best you can be, you have to be willing to risk it all.

Marathon Strong

"Don't you give up on me, five eight three! You are not a quitter, five eight three!"

While I am not, nor probably will ever be, a qualified racer for the Boston Marathon, I deeply admire those who take part. I also admire the fans. It is because the fans, the friends, family, and volunteers who transform marathons or other races from terribly long runs into events.

Marathons take a while to complete. Marathons hosted in cities other than Boston can take even longer as the racers aren't nearly as fast.

As a spectator, there is very little you can do while you wait for your runner of choice to cross the finish line. Unless your runner is equipped with a personal fitness tracking device (thank you Endomodo friend maps) you can only guess your runner's time based on past performance.

Rather than wandering off to a coffee shop or taking an early morning nap propped up against the barricade rails, most spectators spend this time shouting encouragements to random runners. While the spectators don't know whether a runner's name is Sue or Bob, their shouts are specific. "Bring it home, four two three! That's it, seven four one, show that pavement who's boss!"

The spectators read the bib numbers off the racers and make sure that racer knows the spectator is calling directly to them. Often this bit of extra attention is all that is needed for a racer to keep up their grueling pace, because they know someone is watching. The practice makes everyone faster.

If you think about it, these spectators are actually encouraging other racers to beat the person they were originally pulling for. In any other sporting event, the fans would be booing the competition, not cheering for them. With marathons, the thing that matters most is that their runner beat his or her personal best, not how they compared to others.

Many of us want to be successful at what we've chosen to do. We've struggled. We've burned the midnight oil. We dedicated ourselves to learning our craft, business, or other chosen skill. Then we get discouraged or feel threatened when we look at how we supposedly rank against the competition.

As a writer, my only competition is someone who has created an identical story to my own. By identical I mean in terms of length, characterization, plot, and design. In short, someone who is violating all U.S. copyright laws.

My competition is not other struggling writers. I enjoy reading others' works and occasionally comment on other blogs with my real thoughts and feelings based on what they have written, not just to plug my own work. The little gesture of recognition might just give them that needed boost towards their own finish line.

Unless your business deals with professional athletics, we need to change our definition of winning. Being marathon strong isn't about how badly you can beat the competition. It's about how well you exceeded your personal and professional goals over an extended period. That's what we should aspire too. We also need to be willing to shout encouragement to others along the way. It is a lesson that has served me often.

I recall the week and day the pandemic arrived in my community. I'd been watching stories of the virus as it took hold in China, France, and Italy. I'd seen video of garbage trucks in other countries being converted into mobile mass disinfection units that sprayed the streets while the rest of the residents remained locked behind their doors under civil order. It was concerning to be sure, but that was happening elsewhere—not here—not at my home. Until one day, it was.

It was Friday the thirteenth, 2020. A date that was unlucky enough all by itself, but also the date of a full moon. We'd also barely adjusted to the time change for Daylight Saving Time, if life wasn't already crazy enough, when rumors started to circulate that a lockdown was coming.

My children's teachers heard the rumors too and had pro-actively stuffed their school bags with enough lessons and supplies to keep them learning for up to three weeks. They thought they were preparing for the worst, but had no idea their worst would prove to barely cover it.

However, they were also optimistic. Mixed among the supplies in my youngest's bag was a note that said the class would get to watch a movie the following Monday and that he specifically had earned the right to wear his pajamas to school as a reward for behavior. That movie day would never come.

I still have that note.

I also have friends in other countries who'd shared stories of what was coming. I wasn't under any impression we were dealing with a twenty-four-hour stomach bug. Nor was my older sister.

We'd seen the stack of worksheets and had decided the pages weren't enough. We then spent our last weekend of freedom before the lockdown at the local homeschool supply store purchasing additional supplemental education content like squirrels hoarding nuts before a long winter.

The announcement came before the weekend was over. There would be no school for at least two weeks.

My sister and I looked up suggested homeschool schedules and set up desks in our separate houses. We stocked up on snacks and non-perishable goods. The toilet paper shortage, however, caught us both by surprise. Nine days later, we'd get another note from the school system—there would be no return to in-person learning until the middle of May, at the earliest.

I may have drunk one or two adult beverages that night.

A reporter from our local paper reached out, curious to hear how me and other area parents were handling the balancing act of school and full-time work. I was honest. If it hadn't been for a series of timers that let my children know when I expected them to be at their desks and when they could goof off, our house might have descended in to madness. As if to illustrate my point, my children and Her Royal Highness took that as their cue to run around the house like maniacs.

Mid-May was a long way off in the future, and with the school year officially ending the first week of June, I had little confidence the schools would re-open to in-person learning that year. My mind was already jumping to summer break. At least I had my workbooks and lesson plans for now, but if camps remained closed, what would I do? What would any of us do?

My interview was recorded on camera. When the footage aired, it was all too easy to detect a frantic edge to my voice. It was difficult not to give up right then and there. After all, Steve Jobs of Apple fame never finished college. Larry Ellison, founder of Oracle, and Michael Dell of Dell Technologies gave up on college too. Heck, even John D. Rockefeller stopped at a high school education. My kids could still achieve success without a pristine transcript.

However, they would need what those people had or have—an internal drive to get the work done even if it wasn't for a grade. They wouldn't get that by watching me throw in the towel or succumb into a sobbing mess the minute our life got hard. So I pushed on. My mental muscles ached trying to keep track of all the school logins. My lungs hurt from the repressed screams against new-age math solving strategies. I did what I could. I focused on putting one figurative foot in front of the other.

We made it past the first milestone. We were no longer completely on our own. Live instruction was added back into the mix, even if it was remote. We made it past the next. Kiddo graduated from elementary school. Where did the time go?

Somehow I managed to keep them occupied, and myself, employed, over the summer and into the fall. And yet . . . and yet . . . no matter how far it seemed I'd come, the finish line remained out of sight.

However, every so often, the local paper would run a story about parenting in the pandemic and its associated challenges. It was as if the universe could sense I was hitting the proverbial wall A photograph of me standing behind a makeshift desk surrounded by worksheets, a model shark, and tower of LEGOs would pop up as the featured image. I guess I was the last person who'd agreed to a photograph in a while. When this happened, my inbox would swell with messages of encouragement and solidarity.

At first, most of those messages were from my mom and my siblings, but then something unexpected happened. My story, but mostly my photograph, got picked up by other newspapers. I started hearing from people from my old hometown and those I'd worked with years ago. The story and picture spread further. I've heard from people who've spotted my photograph as far as Utah, over two thousand miles, or thirty-four hundred kilometers away.

I will say it's not a flattering image. The room is a mess. I'm frayed around the edges with strands of hair escaping from my ponytail. Nor is it shot from my most attractive angle. However, it is also a picture of my determined best—the moment I willed myself to be marathon strong.

As of this writing, my marathon is not over. I still haven't even seen the finish line in the distance. And yet, the swell of crowd noise—the messages I've received of solidarity and encouragement—makes it feel as if I am getting closer to the end every day, even if I still have a long way to go. It also reminds me I am not alone in this race.

We have all been pushing ourselves beyond the limits of what we previously thought we could endure at some point, and yet many of us have no choice but to press on. We all have it in us to be marathon strong. We just need the occasional encouragement along the way.

So, for anyone who might need to hear it, don't you give up on me, five eight three! You've got this. See you at the finish line.

Adventures in Goal Setting

*B*efore I had children, my work sent me to Hong Kong for eight weeks. During this time, I was housed in a hotel room only a few train stops from the office. I couldn't speak the language. I couldn't even read it. My days were my friends and family's nights back home and vice versa. Millions of people surrounded me and yet was alone.

I arrived in early summer, and it rained almost daily over the first several weeks. My hotel only offered three English-speaking television channels. I was barely over my jet lag and already I could tell that this was going to be a long trip.

Then things began to happen. First my younger sister, who was working second shift at the time, discovered that she and I could fit in a virtual game of cribbage before I went to sleep and before she had to go into the office. We would set up a private table and chat about nothing while pegs moved across the screen. She usually won, but then again, she usually wins when we play in real life. That's always been her game. To me it was like we were living back at home with our parents and every night was game night. The routine combined with regular Skype calls to the hubby helped keep my spirits up.

Then I received an email from my grandfather. I responded back. He marveled his message could reach the other side of the world within minutes of sending. He wanted to know all sorts of mundane details about life in the eastern hemisphere. He would ask questions like: how much is a gallon of gas?

I didn't drive. I only took the subway or the bus and had no reason to know the answer to his question, but it was my grandpa asking. He didn't really expect an instantaneous answer. I could have searched the internet for a quick reply, but I had more than a little time to myself and decided to explore and find out the answer firsthand.

It turns out that gas stations are not exactly easy to find in a land dominated by effective public transit. I could only find one through determination and willingness to get slightly lost. Once located, the sign advertised the price in terms of Hong Kong dollars per liter instead of dollars per gallon. Ah, math . . . The entire exercise reminded me of the word problems we had to solve in school.

I proudly worked out the conversions and hit the reply button. Within a day, Grandpa sent me follow-up questions. I felt I had somehow entered the world's widest-spanning scavenger hunt.

I got my work done throughout my stay, but in addition, I must have crossed the length of the island on foot at least twice. I saw temples and markets. I watched as dragon boats raced across the water. I biked along the shore of the new territories. I enjoyed the Hong Kongese take on barbecue at the home of one of my local colleagues. I even managed to win a few games of cribbage.

The internet has made the world smaller. It allowed me to maintain connections on the other side of the planet, and may have even strengthened those connections. But at the same time, my time over there would have been sorely limited had I remained isolated in my hotel room.

My grandfather taught me a lot in those few weeks about effective goal setting, whether the goal be for personal or professional development.

I've been in the management world long enough to know that goals should be SMART: **S**pecific, **M**easurable, **A**ttainable, **R**elevant, and **T**ime-bound.

Specific—all I had to do was send an email with the cost of gas. Measurable—I sent the email, or I didn't.

Attainable, but not necessarily easy. Goals should force a stretch or other small change in behavior, but not so large a stretch that a person becomes immediately discouraged. In order to complete my goal, I had to leave my hotel. Relevant—the goal's completion should be worthwhile. It should be valued by the person who created it and by the person doing the work. Learning how to operate a computer was a major accomplishment for my grandfather. If he wanted to know the cost of gas, well then, I was going to find it out for him. Time-bound—I couldn't leave him waiting by his machine for an unanswered email. I had to find out the answer before I departed.

Grandpa, whether you find this on your own or mom reads it to you, thanks again for the adventure.

Mountain High

We introduced Her Royal Highness to water. She's a mix breed, but at least part of her noble ancestry can be traced to Labrador. As a result, she deemed that this introduction most pleasing (almost as pleasing as pillows, which she will tell you, remain at stock levels well beneath her station). Therefore, when we received an invitation to a friend's house at a nearby lake, she sent her acceptance post-haste.

Being the highly trained servants we are, we prepared her luggage, which included a bag filled with assorted balls designed for retrieving from lakes or oceans. When we arrived at our destination, she eagerly inspected the property. She sniffed. It would do.

While the front yard is relatively flat, like many other houses on this lake, the house sits well above the water's edge, the ground in the back, with its steep decline more cliff than yard. The land further dropped away under the water. Without a beach or even shallows, to speak of the owners expressed their concerns about playing games such as fetch from the home's pier. "She won't be able to get out on her own," and "you will have to pull her out."

Undeterred by troublesome things like risk, or topography, Her Royal Highness made her way to the bottom of the hill where she waited for her servants to attend her. Splash. Her Royal Highness leaped into the water and began paddling. She turned and looked at those of us standing on the platform. She swam. Then she was gone.

I scanned the area, spotting her moments later on the rocks at the lake's edge. The only problem was the rocks weren't anywhere near the access platform. Her Royal Highness pressed on. I watched, more than a little concerned, as she scaled the hill. Her claws digging into the mud. I wondered as she somehow fit her body between the dirt and a tree, giving herself more leverage. She reached the platform, but unfortunately, its wooden planks were still well above her head. The ground should have been too steep for her to use as an effective launch pad, but launch she did.

I'd gone to the platform intending to haul her up as our friends suggested. I hadn't needed to. The concerns of man (or woman) had not registered in her ears. She crawled up on the platform. Dropping the ball, she wagged her tail and ran back toward the water, leaving muddy paw prints in her path. "Yeah, I don't think this is a good idea," I told her as I picked up the ball. I tried to put it away. After that athletic displayed, she'd earned a rest.

She disagreed.

Splash. Once again, she was in the water.

Over and over she repeated the process. Each time, I thought for sure she'd had enough and each time she proved me wrong. Soon she was finding another way to launch herself. Instead of scaling the hill, she found another rock at the bottom, positioned close to another edge of the pier and would jump from there. Sometimes she would miss. Sometimes she fell down. But she never stopped trying. There is no place for the word 'can't' in Her Royal Highness' kingdom.

I'm not sure who first said it—Confucius, George Bernard Shaw, or Elbert Hubbard, but the saying, "The man who begins to say it can't be done is often interrupted by somebody else doing it," is definitely true.

They say that people eventually resemble their pets. With regards to Her Royal Highness, I find it no insult. At the time of this story, I'd all but written the words 'End of Book Two' in my current draft in process. I've written before about how writing a novel is much like running a marathon and how impossible reaching the finish line can feel when you are at the base of a particularly big hill (or at a lull in the story's progress). As of that day, I'd written over seventy thousand words (that's equivalent to two hundred eighty book pages for my non-writer readers). And that's just this last book. I've written approximately half a million words now when you look at all my publications.

Somedays the words came easily, but not every day. Somedays I had to jump from questionable surfaces, get my hands dirty, and scale seemingly impossible walls. I did this because I have a goal in mind and the confidence and determination to see it through. I am the only thing that can stop me. All that suggests otherwise is noise.

Harder, Better, Faster, Stronger

One afternoon, years upon years ago, I picked up my then toddler from daycare as I normally did, but this afternoon was special. His teacher approached me positively beaming. "He attempted to climb out of his bed today at nap time," she explained with a big grin. Though he sleeps in a big boy bed at home, his bed at daycare is one of those portable cribs. To my eyes, there is a fairly significant drop from the railing to the floor below. For many caregivers, reporting that a child in their care is putting themselves into a potentially harmful situation isn't something to be excited about. At least it isn't something to be positively excited about.

But my little lord tyrant has always had a way of redefining expectations.

My son has hyper-mobility, which has become a less pronounced trait over time, but at the time had made it difficult for him to catch up to his peers in terms of motor skills. If that challenge hadn't been bad enough, according to his last several check-ups, it was likely to inherit his height from my side of the gene pool. Poor thing. My height hasn't been considered average since before the 1900s. The crib wall came up to his shoulders. Therefore, if he was able to successful pull his entire body weight over that height, it was an impressive achievement, even if earned him a few new bruises as a trophy.

The conversation reminded me about the multiple weeks we spent with the physical therapist. Once he achieved walking, each follow-up appointment started by placing him on a baby treadmill. His therapist explained to me that in order to build up muscle mass in his legs, he had to first tire them out. He had to make his muscles strain and suffer in order to build up their strength. The phrase no pain, no gain, came to mind.

Pain is a funny thing. It warns us when there is something the matter so that changes can be made before more permanent damage is done. Without the sensation of pain, you might not realize you need to remove your hand from a hot pan on the stove. If we are lucky, an unexplained pain can send us to the doctor before a tumor becomes untreatable. While pain is something most of us would like to avoid, it is a necessary component to continued health.

Pain can also be the world's best teacher. If we never experienced hurt, and life's other lows, we would never truly be able to fully appreciate their opposites. If we never pushed ourselves to our limits, we would never fully learn the extent of our capabilities.

I'd begun work on a new novel around this same time. However, with each project the task had become increasingly more complicated to execute. This was because success in the publishing world tends to require you to do multiple things at once. I was also in the process of editing another book and planned to release a new edition in the coming months. I also still had to finalize cover designs and begin rolling out that book's release. Finding the time to fit in the writing of a new novel then was no easy feat.

But in some ways, writing it was significantly easier than writing my first books. This book was a sequel. This gave me an edge. I knew these characters and their setting. I also knew what it took to pull their story from my mind and put it to paper. As a result, I thought I would be able to plan my schedule accordingly and thought I had given myself a pretty healthy runway. It later proved I needed more time to do right by my story. During this time, I often felt as if I was straining myself, trying to do so much, but in the end it made my determination to succeed that much stronger.

This was because I recognized I was asking my toddler to continue to push himself week after week, and he was rising to the occasion. The least I could do, then was to do the same. So I buckled down. I pushed myself through the mountain of work and finished one project and moved on to the next. I thought I'd learned to understand and accept the benefits of pain.

My youngest grew older. His skills increased and soon he no longer needed to see a physical therapist. Instead, he saw more friends. He attended more playdates. He was invited to more parties.

A few years later, he was invited to attend a sports-themed party at a local gym. As part of its birthday party package, the facility provided instructors who would lead the kids in several games. They played rounds of baseball, dodgeball, and soccer all in a matter of minutes while parents watched from the wings.

Most of the kids appeared to be having a wonderful time. However, as the party progressed, I watched my son's expression transform from one of joy to greater frustration and sorrow with each activity. He wasn't as fast as the other kids. His swings of the baseball bat hit mostly air. His kicks failed to get the ball past the goalie.

He was tiring while the other kids were just getting started.

My son may have been experiencing muscle fatigue or other physical pain, but he was also experiencing something that can hurt just as much, if not worse—the pain of being different. I knew it would happen one day—we're all different, after all. It just is easier to accept when you are older. It also broke my heart to see it happen and not be able to do a thing about it.

The other kids weren't making fun of him. I doubt most any of them even noticed. He wasn't being asked to sit out a game. He wasn't being excluded, at least he wasn't being excluded by his peers. Instead, he gradually excluded himself from play. He'd linger by the parents' area. He stayed well behind the starting line. I watched as he gave up. My heart broke a little more.

He claimed he needed a water break and came over to my side. His eyes shone under the overhead lights. Tears had not yet filled them, but they were forming. "I suck," my son said to me.

"No, you don't," I assured him.

"I'm not good at anything," he said.

"You are good at plenty of things," I said. I rattled off the list of talents, his artistic skills, his caring heart, his quick wit, and ready laugh.

"But not sports," he said.

"You just need more practice," I told him. It was also true. I realized that while we'd sent his brother to soccer classes years before we sent him to school, and were now attending his baseball games, we hadn't done the same for the child standing in front of me.

The party planners must have sensed that something was the matter as they took that moment to invite parents to join in the next game. I took his hand. "Let's give it one more try." His face made it clear that he had no confidence this time would be any different from the last, but followed me back into the main room.

The planners announced this round would be another variation of dodgeball—kids versus grown-ups. I caught my youngest's eye. "You're going down, kid."

"Oh no, I'm not," he said.

The good luck fairy must have waved her magic wand over my son's ball, because no matter how much I shouted I was going to win this round, my youngest's throws hit their intended target—me. His aim was uncanny. He also somehow evaded all of my return volleys. They kept going wide. In fact, the ball seemed to miss all the kids in the room no matter who threw it. It only connected with the parents. Within minutes anyone old enough to vote was sitting on the floor—out, while all the kids ran around and cheered. Funny how that happened.

Light and laughter returned to my little boy's eyes. Mastering various sports might be harder for him as he grows up. He might not be faster or stronger than the other participants on the court or field, but in this moment he was the same as his peers. A kid who'd gotten the better of his mother—just like all the others. He'd doubted the outcome, but had taken part anyway because we were there and he knew that, if nothing else, we had each other. Did he suspect his team may have had an additional advantage contributing to the indisputable victory? If so, it didn't matter to him. He'd tried his best and had succeeded. The moment itself, it would seem, was enough of a win for both of us.

Friendly Neighborhood Spider-Man

The line to get into the gym after New Year's resembled a nightclub as I pulled into the parking lot. The only difference was the women waiting to get in were clad in tight-fitting neon (yet perfectly coordinated) active-wear rather than the little black dress. Without intending to, I looked at my gym bag. All I had packed was my usual garb: a pair of stretchy pants, comfortable shoes, and a loose (but breathable) shirt. I'd missed the memo.

I made my way through the crowd and into the hall o'cardio. It is a massive room with rows of equipment. Usually, there are plenty spots available, but today it was packed to near capacity. I was going to have to make do with whatever was free, which likely meant I would be stuck on the machine with the squeaky gear and poor ear bud connection. Sure, there are far worse problems to have, but annoying sounds are like kryptonite for my exercise motivation (as are a lot of things).

Sure enough, even though the room was crowded, Ye Olde squeaker just happened to be available. *Lucky me*. Passing some full-length mirrors along the way, I noticed my reflection. It was difficult to repress a sigh at what I saw. I don't consider myself exceptionally large for my frame, but I could drop five (or a dozen) pounds without people worrying if I was eating enough. While I haven't yet completely surrendered to their call, I now understand why 'mom jeans' exist. *Thanks, kids*.

As I mounted Ye Olde Squeaker and keyed up the day's torture program, I found myself looking for my friendly neighborhood Spider-Man. No, I don't mean the web crawler from the comics. I mean a large full-grown adult male who comes to the gym clad in a short-sleeved, short-legged, skin-tight Spider-Man outfit.

I'd noticed him almost immediately when I began attending the gym. After all, it was hard not to. At first, I almost felt sorry for him for being that clueless. Then, I wondered if he lost a bet, but I saw him again the following week in the same outfit and again the next. If it was a bet, it was a big one.

This cycle repeated at least once a week throughout the year. I would go to the gym and Spider-Man would be there too. Over time, I realized I had grown to expect a sighting of this fashion disaster with each visit. Once spotted, I'd feel a little better about my own choices, which made it easier to power through my workout with gusto. (Okay, gusto may be a stretch, but at least, I felt good enough about my performance afterward to return another day.) Eventually, though, I realized I'd even come to respect Spider-Man. He, clearly, was a person who did not care what anyone else thought. Instead of thinking he looked ridiculous, I now wished I could be half as confident.

But there was no sign of him during the first week of the new year among the horde of toned bodies. Bodies which I could only guess were only there because they were on the payroll of some brand of active-wear, hired to act as living models, or the gym paid them to entice members into signing up for additional services. I glanced again at my reflection as my finger lingered over the start button. I saw my well-worn sweats and at my extra curves that refused to quit and thought, why was I bothering? I felt my resolve crumble.

Stop it, Allie.

You have two options: You can use your hour of 'me time' the way you intended to or you can go home and chase after boys who have been housebound due to rain over the last several days. *Good Point Allie.*

I told myself to ignore the crowd, at least this once. I rationalized most of them wouldn't be around for long. A quarter would give up their resolutions before the end of February. Another group would likely drop in April when the weather starts to warm and there are actual things to do outside. I cranked up the volume on my phone and got to work.

Suddenly it hit me. I knew it wasn't going to be crowded long because I'd been going to the gym regularly for months. I was no resolution mayfly (my waistline isn't the only part about me that is stubborn). I remembered the real reason I was there (me—curves and all). I gave it all I had. Afterward, Ye Olde Squeaker proudly displayed my accomplishment—one of my personal bests. I rowed and used the free weights too. In short, I rocked my workout that afternoon.

I may not be model fit. I may be under-tall. But I'll face my goals and power through another year. Who knows, maybe one day I might even be like Spider-Man too.

After all—Spider-Man, Spider-Man, does whatever a spider can.

Life Isn't a Spectator Sport

My youngest son was late with all of his motor development milestones: crawling, sitting upright, even rolling over. When he was late walking, we just assumed he just wasn't ready and was taking his time. It was par for the course with him. We joked he was a lazy bum. We were concerned, but not worried.

I repeated that same joke in the doctor's hearing during one of my son's pediatric check-ups. It was around the one-year-old mark. Unlike me, the doctor didn't find it nearly as funny, especially not after taking a longer view at my son's development charts. Within minutes, I had a referral in hand to see a physical therapist.

I would have liked to have said I scheduled the appointment with the therapist the same day. Instead, I placed the note to the side of my desk and continued on as I had before. I convinced myself that if I just gave my son another day, he would suddenly master the skill all on his own. My son was perfectly healthy. Every kid and every kid's development is different. There was nothing to worry about.

A month passed with no progress. When I finally gave in and dialed the therapist's number, it felt like I was admitting defeat, as if I was giving up on my child, but I decided a second opinion couldn't hurt. Ever positive, I told myself that the therapist would examine him and tell me he just needed more time. We would only be out the cost of an office visit. No big deal.

It didn't happen that way. Instead, that's when we were told that our son has a condition known as hypermobility and low muscle tone. What this means is that because of additional extreme flexibility in his joints, he is going to have to work at least twice as hard as any other kid to do anything requiring movement. Any movement—walking, chewing—you name it. This pronouncement was a little hard to take. Yes, she could have told us that the cause for his delayed development was something much scarier, but it's difficult to hear that your baby is in some way flawed (on paper), no matter the diagnosis.

We started seeing the therapist weekly. It was as if he had just been in need of the proper key to unlock all the secrets of the world. Never satisfied with his current status, she forced him to build another skill on each minor accomplishment. With her help, he began crawling without dragging his body on the floor. Then he began pulling himself upright and taking tentative first steps and walking at eighteen months. We wanted to throw a parade with each milestone. Instead, his therapist merely moved on to the next skill.

As a result, a year later, he was running, climbing, and otherwise finding ways to turn my brown hair gray. He'd practically caught up with others his age and was no longer in weekly therapy. Yes, he tired more quickly than others, but you wouldn't know it, watching him chase after his brother with a big smile on his face.

I don't have many regrets, but not scheduling that first appointment sooner is right up there.

I didn't want to admit to myself that there might be a problem, and so I ignored the nagging voice telling me that something wasn't right. I thought time itself was enough to mend all things. I thought everything would work itself out, and everyone would be happy if I just left well enough alone.

I've never been so wrong.

I have to acknowledge that I wasn't a coach or a leader back then. At least not at home. I was too far in denial. Yes, I was creating a vision of a brighter future for my family, but I wasn't setting a course for how we would get there. "Wait and See" is a tactic, not a strategy. Nor was I providing my son with the tools he needed to learn on his own.

I wasn't a supporting teammate either. Followers like these may not set the game plan, but at least they actively take part in executing on the win. No, I was only a spectator. I was hoping for the best, cheering from the sidelines, but my passive watching and waiting would never score points in life's big game.

For a year of his life, my son's potential was untapped. But luckily it didn't have to stay that way. All we had to do to get us both back into the game was to make that first call.

One Foot Forward

"Are you combing your hair with your toes?" is a question I never thought I would need to ask, but when your child is the human incarnate of a Gumby doll, I guess anything goes.

My youngest, LT, as I've mentioned before, has hyper-mobility. It is a condition that allows him to perform fun party tricks like the one above, but made it difficult to build up the muscle definition needed to sit up, crawl, or walk. He spent almost a year of his life in physical therapy mastering skills which other kids picked up naturally at a half (or a third) of his age. It seemed he would never gain the knack, until one day the pieces fell into place, and he took his first step.

It was nearly time for him to take his next first step—into kindergarten.

To say that I was a wee bit nervous is an understatement. Thus far he had spent his entire life surrounded by those who have known him, his abilities, and his limitations from birth. But once he passed through the doors of the school, he'd be in a classroom of twelve to twenty children, each with unique talents and challenges of their own. He'd made significant progress since finally taking that first step, but had it been enough? Had he caught up to his peers? If not, how would he cope? How would his teacher? We would soon find out.

As the last days of the 2017 summer break wound down a group of us (eight adults, six children under the age of ten, and two dogs) decided to head to the Outer Banks, which is a series of naturally forming islands off the coast of North Carolina where pirates once sailed and wild horses still roam.

After two days of red flags, which signify a dangerous riptide in the water, we decided to take in the surrounding sights and made our way to the Currituck Beach Light.

Currituck's lighthouse is not the tallest lighthouse in North Carolina, at one hundred ninety-eight point five feet (sixty point five meters) that distinction goes to the lighthouse at Cape Hatteras, but it would do.

The sun beat down on us as we waited in line. Sweat formed as the staff advised it would be another twenty to thirty minutes' wait before we could go inside. The kids scattered across the green while the adults held their places. I watched as my eldest and one of his cousins started playing tag. LT attempted to join in but he couldn't compete with their speed and soon the game lost its appeal.

LT returned to my side and guzzled down the contents of my only remaining bottle of water, already showing signs of tiring. I looked at the tower. Two hundred twenty spiraling steps awaited us, constructed prior to any form of building safety code (or air-conditioning). Some of our group discussed sitting this one out as the crowd waiting increased along with the temperature. I looked at LT. He was small, but there was no way I would be able to carry him to the top were he to slip or give up mid-climb.

The line moved. Our group was next. It was time to decide who was going and who was staying on the ground. LT didn't hesitate to join his brother and cousins at the front of the line. His face was set. His decision was made. I guess mine was too.

The majority of our group disappeared up the stairs within seconds of our entry. I hung back, ready to react as I could as my youngest grabbed the handrail and took that first step forward. I watched with laser focus as he took another. Then another. We reached the landing at the top of the first flight of stairs. Eight more flights to go.

LT didn't look back. We rounded the next. The inside of the tower narrowed.

Halfway up, another group appeared at the top of the next landing and began their descent. I made the mistake of glancing down. It was all too easy to imagine what might happen if LT were to slip now. Maybe it would be best for us to stop and wait with our backs against the wall while they squeezed past. I hesitated. LT did not. Instead, he kept climbing.

We met more and more people the higher we went and each time my stomach twisted along with my heart, but LT never looked back, never complained, never asked me to do the work for him, and never once stopped.

Then we were at the top of the stairs and roughly one hundred fifty feet (slightly more than forty-five meters) from the ground. A small doorway through the brick wall opened to an external landing, which circled the lighthouse and provided an unencumbered view of both the ocean and the sound separating the island from the mainland. But the most beautiful sight for me was the smile on LT's face as he joined the rest of our family on the rail.

It was enough to make me forget we had to still go back down. Well . . . almost.

We reached the bottom with LT leading the line of children behind me. After exiting, I turned and looked up once more, amazed again at how far this one little guy had gone on his own and reminded once more of how much can be accomplished one determined step at a time.

How would he cope with this next stage in his life or any goal he sets his mind to for that matter? I had my answer. It was the same way any of us should—with one foot forward.

Get a Grip

The outside temperature had fallen, but still could be described as fitting into a range between volcanic rim and Amazonian jungle. Unfortunately, Her Royal Highness, my dog, requires daily inspections of her kingdom, no matter the weather. Within seconds of exiting the house, the soles of my flip-flops were slick from the trapped humidity. Still, temperatures aside, it was a beautiful day for a walk and Her Royal Highness was happy enough to trot along by my side.

As we rounded the corner, I noticed a group of teenagers on bicycles approaching. I raised my hand in greeting. As one girl passed, she politely said hello. I was thinking to myself what nice kids when WHAM! The next thing I knew I was experiencing the joy of flight. My arm was nearly pulled out of its socket while my feet simultaneously left the ground. Unfortunately, my air time was only short-lived as I found myself next lying on my back in the grassy area that separates sidewalk from street looking up at a blue sky.

Able to pull trains and leap buildings in a single bound, it's Wonder Dog!

Whimper . . . *blink blink*. Owie . . . It turned out that Her Royal Highness, having noticed me greet the teenagers, decided it would be a grand idea to introduce herself to them as well. Without delay. So what if they were now already several yards away? Her Royal Highness typically has impeccable manners and so now and then I forget that she also has the natural strength to hoist the remains of the Titanic off the seabed floor and the speed of a cheetah running from a bee sting. She was kind enough to remind me. She'd taken off at full tilt, ignoring the minor detail that we were still technically attached.

As feeling returned to my arm, I realized that the leash somehow remained gripped firmly in my hand. I had remained strong, even though the same could not be said about gravity. I felt the grass by my side as attempted to sit up and had to wonder at my luck to land in the soft earth when my head could have, should have come in contact with the concrete of the sidewalk.

One girl shouted from up the hill, "Are you okay?" I guess they'd witnessed my amazing aerial acrobatics and pulled over to assess the situation.

"I'm fine," I replied as my dog returned to my side and began licking my face. "But she may not be," I joked as I rubbed Her Royal Highness' head with my good hand to assure her I was okay while attempting to look stern and scolding. I turned the leash over as I regained my footing. I realized that hadn't been a polite response. Though there was still a dull ache in my arm, overall I was okay. Why wasn't my skull now cracked on the ground much like Humpty Dumpty?

I hadn't let go.

If my hand had only held the leash loosely, I'd have let go at the initial snap. I might not have lost my footing, but my furry companion could have successfully reached those polite kids on their bikes and who knows what sort of injuries might have resulted. If I had let go the minute, I realized my feet were parallel to my head, I may well be writing this from a hospital bed. But I hadn't, and because we were still attached, the momentous force that is Her Royal Highness on a mission carried my airborne body just far enough away from the sidewalk to land in the grass with only a minor scrape to show for my experience.

Of course, I would have preferred not to fall at all, but her majesty had been a stray until February of that year and the occasional mistake was still to be forgiven. Although, even if she'd been with us since a pup and had years rather than weeks of training, I know a mistake could still happen. No path is without the occasional ill-advised temptation or other misfortune. The point is, that when these speed bumps happen, you have to keep your grip on that which matters most. While your world may, for a time, seem upside down, if you hold on long enough, you too might just find yourself landing safety.

The Tale of Two Vines

Mary, Mary, quite contrary, how does your garden grow?

Ignoring the fact that my name isn't Mary, nor do I consider myself contrary (well—at least, not most of the time), my garden might have looked better in prior years, but was at least back in bloom. A few weeks prior to this story, I wasn't sure that would be the case.

February and March had been rather dramatic months weather-wise with temperature fluctuations that were extreme even for North Carolinian standards. One day would be warm enough to turn on the air-conditioning and let the kids run outside in their swimsuits—the next day cold enough to pull out the parkas. I'd fallen ill as a result, but was finally starting to feel well enough to rejoin the outside world.

Our news reported that much of the commercial plant life was equally confused by the temperature fluctuations and budded too early. This would cause several crops to be considered a total loss after the frost returned. The local farmers had to be devastated. I was bummed too. Not only would produce be more expensive that year, but I feared it also would jeopardize our annual family strawberries picking in May. Therefore, I was delighted to notice green leaves and white flowers on the vines that grow in my backyard (kids there's hope for us yet).

For the past several years, I'd grown grapes as well as blackberries, among a few other foodstuffs in my garden, but though they grow side by side, the vines are as different as people.

My blackberries, for example, barely needed to be covered in earth before they took off on their own, with several shoots of new vines popping up in other beds independent of my plantings. My grapes, on the other hand, required a little more attention.

The first year we were together, the vines grew, but never produced. The second was more of the same. I considered letting the blackberries take over, but decided to give them one more chance while doing a bit more homework.

I think, in this case, my plants appreciated the phone-a-friend rather than my undivided attention. I learned a while back that grapevines produce best when pruned while the weather is still cold and the plants are dormant. In my area, that means late February.

I remember the first time I clipped away at the vines (which look more branch-like than vine-like at that time of year). I thought to myself how the practice must seem to the plant. Here they were, having barely survived the harshness of winter, they then forced to suffer further as their limbs were hacked away.

During such times, I imagine that if my grapes were people, they might cry at how unfair their life was compared to that of the blackberry. If they were religious fruit, they might also wonder if they were being tested and rage against their gardener. I understand what it must seem like for them, but still, I continue snipping away in the cold of winter year after year, not because of some cruel game, but because I care. I do this so that when summer finally arrives, they will be the best they can be.

And when summer does arrive, the situation in my garden is quite different. My blackberries, having produced small clusters of berries in the spring, are only shadows of their former glory. Several of the vines, hunched over, touching the ground under the weight their leaves, as small as they are, are more brown than green and most vines will be forced to give away to the next generation of shoots now breaking through the dirt's surface on either side.

My grapevines, however, remain strong even under the weight of heavy bunches of fruit. The fruit itself will be protected from the cruel sun by gorgeous full leaves wider than a hand-span or two, but not so protected they cannot ripen fully thanks to their vine's earlier sacrifice. Meanwhile, tendrils of new vines, still growing, will stretch and twist around nearby surfaces, as much the bully in their newfound success as the blackberry once was.

The point is my grapevine should not envy my blackberry for its easy start (as tempting as that might be at the time). The grapevine that experienced and overcame hardship will bear fruit much longer. It will be made stronger in a way the blackberry, by its very nature, will never appreciate nor understand. That grapevine will become capable of withstanding the next extreme with a confidence felt to its roots, returning year after year in steady growth, while others might rise quickly only to fall. It's a lesson, and eventual outcome, I try to keep in mind when dealing with my own hardship or two.

While both plants produce their own delicious fruit in their own season, in terms of success per individual vine, there really is no comparison.

How I Almost Lost My Feet to Save My Face

When I was a teenager I almost lost both of my feet. No. I don't mean I stumbled, or lost my footing. I mean, I was at risk of my feet being potentially cut off. Gone. Bye-bye.

I wasn't particularly religious, but I enjoyed spending time with my church youth group. They were a fun bunch (it also didn't hurt that a couple of guys were easy on the eye), and it was an excuse to hang out with people my age without parents or homework. The group I belonged to regularly took part in a summer day camp program for underprivileged children in the Appalachian mountains. We would travel to the primary site where we would join other groups from various denominations and creeds, and get sorted into smaller mixed teams. During the day, our small groups would go to nearby sister facilities to act as counselors and chauffeurs for the kids. At night, we would rejoin the large group and sleep in large wooded cabins.

I started to pack my bag. I had a problem. The terrain required closed-toed shoes, and I had nothing suitable. My boots were designed for winter. I'd bake. My summer footwear was typically either sandals or nothing at all. I had to go last-minute shopping. I was in a rush, but I still wanted to look somewhat cool. I got a pair of low-cut Chuck Taylor knock-offs. The back of the shoe was stiff and rubbed the top of my heel, but I knew the shoe just needed to be broken in properly. No big deal. I threw a handful of socks into my bag along with the rest of my clothes. I was ready to go.

Even with the socks, my new shoes rubbed my heels to the point of blisters within the first hours of our departure. I knew that nothing much could be done about it, so I didn't complain.

We arrived at the site. It rained. It rained some more. There was no point in trying to stay dry, everything, and everyone was soon waterlogged. As we didn't have dryers at the cabin, all you could do was change into what dry clothes remained while your wet things hung to air dry from any available surface. I had worn all of my socks by the end of the second day and had started a system of drying them, turning them inside out, and using them again. Desperate times.

I noticed that my shoes were getting tighter. I figured they were shrinking due to the wet conditions. My feet started hurting all the time. I would smile and laugh with the kids during the day, but secretly hope they wouldn't ask for a game of tag. A couple of days later, as I pulled off my shoes and wet socks, I saw my feet were the size of an elephant's, swollen, discolored, and oh how they reeked! The blisters had popped and in their place were weeping sores. Painful yes, but ew! I quickly pulled on another recycled pair of air-dried socks. I definitely did not want anyone to see my feet like this. I didn't want to be labeled as gross. Mom would know what to do when I got home.

At this point I was complaining to a few close friends about how much my feet hurt and begun to waddle, but camp would end soon. I was telling, but I was definitely not showing. Once I got home, I would burn those shoes and all would be better. I told myself, think of the children. What's a few more days of discomfort. We were the highlight of their summer. Keep it in perspective. The rain finally tapered off.

It was finally the last night of camp. All the children had celebrated and gone back home. Only the various groups remained. We had one last group bonfire. At the end, the camp's organizer asked us to get into small groups and reflect upon the last several days. A man from another church standing nearby turned to me a put me on the spot. He asked me to start us off with a prayer. I completely panicked. Sure, I knew the ritual ones, how to ask for blessings for food and family and whatnot, but I just didn't do freestyle prayer, at least not out loud, and especially not with strangers! I said a few other words, but then blurted out that I just wanted my feet to stop hurting. Mortified, I apologized for my lack of skill. The man smiled and said that was enough. It was the next person's turn.

I hobbled back to my cabin. Still coping from my embarrassment, I yanked off my shoes and socks and showed my feet to one of the other adults in the room as if to justify why I was complaining during the time that should have been spent on positive reflection. "See! See!" Her face dropped. "We need to get you to hospital . . . Now."

The doctor informed me that had I waited much longer to seek treatment, the gangrene would have taken my feet. My prayer would have been answered, although not quite as I would have liked. My feet would only hurt as phantoms. It's a reminder to be careful what you wish for. As it was, the infection was still treatable and while I still have small scars on both heels, I can still walk just fine on my own two feet.

Whether you want to believe it was the prayer that put those people in front of me or prefer lucky coincidence, my finally speaking up was what made the key difference in the final outcome. From that experience, I learned the value of packing proper footwear (sorry — comfort now trumps fashion for me), but more importantly that I needed to stop letting my worries about what people might think about me from keeping me from asking for or accepting help.

An Unexpected Lesson on Never Giving Up

I elected to take AP English in my last year of high school. For those not as familiar with the American educational system, an AP class was an advanced course offered by some high schools that could translated into university credits depending on your score on the final exam. It's a nice benefit, provided you are willing to do the work. But it is a lot of work.

It was clear from the very first second I stepped into that classroom that this course was not going to be like the English courses I'd taken in school years past. The cinder-block walls that made up the main buildings of my school's campus, were painted in a mural of literary characters. It was bright and glaring and took a while for my eyes to adjust looking at all that color considering all the other walls around campus were stark white.

The class was barely underway when our teacher began handing out a list of books we would not only be required to read in addition to our regular coursework, we'd be also expected to analyze. I remember thinking repeatedly as she rattled off more titles—what have I gotten myself into?

The question only grew louder in my brain as the class stretched on. I thought of the rest of my schedule and the demands of my other courses. Classes like science and math. Classes, which I thought would have a greater impact on my future career.

You could still ask to change your schedule during the first two weeks of school, and so after the second class, I approached my teacher to tell her that as much as I liked her style, I worried I would be overwhelmed and would she mind signing my transfer request.

My teacher listened to my concerns but didn't pick up her pen. Instead, she looked me in the eye and told me she thought I had what it took. She asked me to think about it a while longer and if at the end of the second week I still wanted to move to another class, she would sign the request without argument. Considering she didn't know me any more than the other students in the class, I wondered briefly if she had said what she had out of some form of self-interest. Would she get dinged for her performance if kids transferred? I wondered. Then again, I argued, she'd probably get dinged more for kids not passing. Wouldn't she? Mostly, though, I found myself wanting to believe what she said. I wanted to be that person she thought I was.

I agreed to her suggestion. In the scheme of things, what really was another day or two?

At the end of the year, we entered the room only to find the mural all but gone, with the majority of walls painted the same white as the rest of the campus. Our teacher explained then that for those final days she wanted us to fill in the blank spaces. She would supply the paint and we could pair up however we wanted, but we were to create a mural of our own based on readings we'd done throughout the year for the next class to enjoy the following year.

I left behind a piece of myself on the walls of that classroom, if only for as long as an extra year, but I took with me much more.

I've blocked out the majority of my high school experience, but not her class, and not the lessons I learned there. For it was there I learned that, while I will be tempted to quit when the work gets difficult or otherwise overwhelming, if I press on, the end result will likely prove to be worth the sweat and tears. I also learned that while I might not always believe in myself, there are others out there who are willing to believe enough for the both of us. The trick is to trust them.

It is important to find mentors in life, people who believe enough in you to coach you through the tough times. A simple nod of encouragement by these people can be enough to make the difference between success and failure. And there is no rule to limit a person to just one. You can build yourself a team of mentors if that's what your path to success requires.

And if you find yourself one day looking into the eyes of someone considering giving up, think of the people who once believed in you. Look them in the eye and tell them to give it another day. Who knows what a difference your words can make.

Fly Robin Fly

People talk about kids leaving the nest all the time, but what they don't always mention is how the momma bird occasionally has to leave the nest too.

In order for her babies to hatch, she too has to survive to warm them. Therefore, it is critical that she spread her wings and brave the unknown in order to ensure everyone, herself included, reach their full potential.

Then once hatched, the baby birds have to eat, but also they need to be shown how to be the best sort of birds. This means, eventually, Momma bird has to get over her fears, remember how to fly, and lead by example.

People aren't all that different. More specifically, I'm not that different.

My nest, however, isn't made of sticks or straw. My nest is a series of jobs I managed to pick up over the years and a career I built up along the way. And I'm not complaining about my nest. The people I've met along the way have been great. I've traveled the world and got to see first-hand how things were made. It gave me opportunities I might never have imagined for myself. I am as proud of what I built as I am of my other accomplishments.

However, my nest no longer fit like it once did. While it still kept the cold out, the straw I'd grown so comfortable in over the years no longer provided the same amount of cushioning. The sticks I'd woven together itched my feathers in ways I couldn't fully explain and the gaps in my nest's construction were no longer something I could ignore.

Just another normal day at the office.

I was left with two options: rebuild it by re-weaving together bits and pieces of my existing nest, hopeful that the results would prove adequate for my needs, or I could take a chance, stretch my wings, and try something new.

An opportunity appeared, and I took it.

I started a new job with a company I've never worked with before rather than simply taking on new responsibilities in the same, familiar organization. It was the first time I'd been able to say that in over fifteen years.

I was frankly terrified. What if I was making a mistake? What if it didn't work out? What if I failed?

I had no way of knowing how these new sticks will fit together or how well they'll prove to keep out the rain, but was excited to say that I've tried. But that's the thing about chances—only time will tell which way they'll go. You have to take them anyway if you ever want to grow.

It was also only the first of a few changes I decided to make.

We'd been considering moving for a number of years—ever since my youngest came home from the hospital when the diaper boxes alone threatened to fill a room, but there was always something. The timing was bad, the lot wasn't right, or the location too far away from our jobs. So we'd put it off and put it off, and put it off.

Though we eventually didn't have to worry about rooms full of diapers, we still had plenty of other clutter to find places for. My husband heard about minimalism and gave it a try, clearing out his closet of all but the essential. He tried to work on mine too—but I'm not quite as committed to the cause.

We found new homes for baby toys, only for the free space to be filled with Hot Wheels. We sold off furniture that wasn't being used. Big boy beds took their place. We got creative with things like Murphy desks and multi-use space. Our kids were inconsiderate enough to continue to keep growing.

But our kids weren't the only things to change over the years—our house started to show its age too. First, the water heater went out. Then there was the indoor waterfall (though in defense of my house, that one wasn't entirely its fault). Then the air conditioner failed—twice. Not to be outdone, the furnace went out too. It was one thing after another. Suddenly, I felt less like I was in my home and more like I'd fallen into the plot of the movie, the Money Pit.

Even so, I loved my house. Or at least, I loved my location. I loved how close we were to the greenway, the series of wooden paths that run through my city where you can go when you need help visualizing what the world might look like after the collapse of civilization. (Necessary research in my case). As much as I wanted more space, part of me didn't ever want to move.

I loved my neighbors and the fact my kids could run out at nine in the morning and be outside all day without me worrying about things like traffic or sketchy individuals. Seeing them play with kids next door and down the street brought back memories of my childhood, back in years we won't mention when the news was a lot less scary. The last thing I wanted was to jeopardize all that.

But I hadn't been the only one in need of more room to stretch my wings. The darn kids kept growing too and no matter how much clutter we were able to offload or rehome, it never seemed to be enough. So, love it or not, we kept an eye out for something else. Then one day, unexpectedly, we found something that checked all the boxes. As much as I hated the idea of moving away from our block, it was a place where I could envision an equally memorable future.

We arranged for movers. A representative walked through our soon-to-be former home and gave us an estimate, saying it wouldn't be too bad as we didn't have all that much. Later he would learn just how wrong he was. It seems that a family can acquire a lot of stuff over the course of fifteen years.

The day of the move came. Our neighbor snapped a picture of the truck leaving, captioning it with a sweet goodbye. However, the joke was on her—we had to come back for three more loads before all was said and done.

I'm mostly unpacked now and have since learned where the new light switches are, but curiously enough, never did find the trusted zero key on my keyboard. The place is starting to feel more like my own. That said, the next time we move, I'll make sure I take more memories with me than clutter.

When All is Said and Done

"You are going to die," kiddo announced rather matter-of-fact the other night as I helped him get ready for bed.

I see. It was time for one of those talks. "Yes, I am," I answered, "but hopefully not anytime soon."

"I am going to live forever," he replied, "because I eat healthy foods."

"So do I kiddo, or at least I try." Okay, so I don't try as hard as he does. Kiddo, has always eaten more healthy than I do. The only craving I had while pregnant with him was for tilapia and asparagus and now his favorite meal is a salad with a balsamic glaze and a side of strawberries. At six-years-old, my eldest son could be a bit of an odd child.

"Then why are you going to die?"

"Because that's what happens when you get older." Preferably much, much older, but unfortunately you can't ever quite count on time. Earlier that year a friend and co-worker was diagnosed with a terminal illness which had progressed beyond treatment. It didn't matter that she was only five years older than me at the time or that one of her sons is near the same age as mine. Her illness neither cared about her age or her children's and took her like a greedy monster.

I hug my children tighter whenever I think of her. I wish we didn't need such stark reminders that every moment is precious.

David Brooks of the New York Times, once asked in an moving and inspiring TED talk, "Should you live for your resume . . ., or your eulogy?" He went on to describe that when asked most people reply that they place a higher value on the virtues they hope their friends and family cite during their eulogy over the accomplishments of their resume. Put differently, when your time comes, do you want your family to announce that you streamlined processes by eighty five percent while meeting and/or exceeding performance goals, or that you never missed a tee-ball game? And yet, the resume accomplishments are what we focus on.

When I began writing, I will admit a driving force was the knowledge that when I was done, I would have something tangible on the shelf with my name on it. I put in the work to prove to myself I had what it takes. Proud as I was of my accomplishment, I gave one of those early copies to the woman who watched my youngest during the day. Afterward, she'd flipped through the pages and saw my children's names in black and white. "You've given them a great gift."

As we talked, I realized she meant I had given them more than just a thing to remember me by. I had ensured that some small piece of them would be remembered too.

I like to think I am teaching my boys resilience, determination, and the importance of hard work, but maybe just maybe when all is said and done I've taught them to dream big, and yet to never forget the value of the small everyday. If I can do that, what other accomplishment do I need?

What more do you?

Bonus STORIES

An Interview With My Muse

FIRST PUBLISHED AUGUST 31, 2017

The air was heavy with procrastination as I heard the door open behind me. I didn't have to turn around to recognize her perfume, a mix of earth and chocolate spice. It could only be Moka. Moka Chino. She spelled her name with a 'k' rather than a 'ch.' She thought it gave her an extra shot of originality. I'd never had the heart to tell her I thought it made me question whether her head was on right.

She sashayed into my office as if it hadn't been years since we last met. Though I tried to keep my expression neutral, I couldn't help drinking in her appearance. "What brings you to the old neighborhood?" I asked as she removed a pair nutmeg shaded glasses, revealing mascara stained eyes underneath.

"It's Latte. She's missing."

Latte was Moka's cousin. Tall and skinny—though just as smooth. I'd met her at one of Moka's parties and we'd spent the next hours in easy conversation. Latte's side of the family wasn't nearly as rich and she'd offered to help with the occasional job or two for whatever change I could spare, which was never much.

It was worth the expense. Her contributions might cause me the occasional heartburn, but they never failed to get results. She was reliable that way. It wasn't like her to disappear without leaving a trace.

"So, can you help me find her?"

A lock of white slipped from her frothy up-do. I fought the urge to inhale her scent, as I helped sweep it back into place. She was bad for my health—some might argue, toxic. It was another reason I'd kept my distance. But I also knew she didn't need to ask. Moka was someone I could never say no to. The problem was, she knew it too.

Latte spent her time between gigs in the editorial department of a local publishing house. It would be my first stop.

"Thanks for agreeing to meet with me," I said to Latte's boss, B.K. Caffé, an enormous man with a complexion as dark as his current expression and crushing arms. I extended my hand.

He didn't take it. "You're late."

"I apologize. I was given the wrong directions in reception. Has anyone ever told you guys that this place is difficult to navigate?"

"You said this was about Latte?"

"Yeah, her cousin says she hasn't seen her in a while. Looked worried."

"Yeah, well, I haven't seen her lately either. Now I've got senior management roasting my beans. I've had to bring my sister's kid on board just to deal with the slush." His scowl deepened as he glared as something or someone behind me. "But now I'm beginning to wonder if I was better off."

I followed his gaze. A kid who must have traded his diaper in for an overpriced suit stood there. From the slicked back hair to golden pinkie ring, he could pass for an extra in the Wolf of Wall Street. He marched across the room like I wasn't there. "We need to talk about my assignment."

"Not now."

"But Uncle B, I really don't think you are recognizing all the benefits I bring to the table. I should be in charge out there."

"And yet I still don't have a publish-ready novel from you, now do I."

"If you'd only listen -"

"We can talk later. Now do the job I'm paying you to do."

The kid left, slamming the office door behind him. "Kid thinks he's bulletproof," B.K. said more to himself than to me, shaking his head.

"So, Latte." I took out my notebook, bringing his attention back to the matter at hand. "You saw her last..."

"Weeks ago. We sent a draft off to beta readers and a crew went out celebrating."

"Including you?"

"Not my scene." He crossed his arms over his chest and leaned back in his chair. "I've been told I can be a bit of a buzz kill." Someone knocked on his door. B.K. looked at his watch. "Are we done? I have a schedule to keep."

"One last question. You wouldn't happen to know where they went to celebrate, would you?"

"Where else: Quotable Potables."

I was familiar with the hot spot. Signs of wear on the bar's exterior were beginning to show. Even so, it still maintained a stable of regular customers thanks to its welcoming atmosphere. I made my way to the back where a makeshift karaoke stage, stood. It was also where I knew I'd find the Pinot Sisters.

They were seated at a nearby table, ready to launch into song the moment the equipment came online. I pulled out a chair and handed them a picture. "I'm looking for a gal named Nila Latte. You didn't happen to see her here recently, did you?"

Both girls had the kind of legs that made you want to laugh or weep but were just as known for their bubbly personalities. Usually, the trick was getting them to stop talking, but neither offered a word. "Yes, you did." I tapped the photo again. "A gal like that, on your turf. Yeah, you noticed."

"We don't remember." Nora, the red head, pushed the photo back at me. "Okay?"

"You don't remember seeing her, or you don't remember what happened that night?"

Gio, the blonde, began to sweat, "She was iced!"

Nora covered her sister's mouth. "We don't know that." Her gaze swiveled around the room as she looked for who else might have overheard Gio's outburst. "Really. We don't. Most nights are a complete blur. Ask anyone."

It was clear the girls were spooked and weren't going to tell me anything more, but they'd given me an idea as to who to talk to next. I left the bar and took a turn down Memory Lane. I'd get to the bottom of this story.

It's my job.

After all, I'm a writer.

The Knock

FIRST PUBLISHED, JULY 19 2018

She knelt on the carpet in her new living room, a big cardboard box in front of her, unwrapping ornaments, photographs, and other mementos. The fan overhead rattled as it spun. She'd congratulated herself after installing it earlier that morning, with a mimosa, celebrating the fact she hadn't called her parents a single time, or worse, her ex-boyfriend. The last thing she needed was to give him an excuse to work his way back into her life.

Unfortunately, she had to concede she hadn't spent long enough verifying its blades were balanced before turning it on. She made a mental note to add fixing that to the ever-growing to-do list.

There was a knock at the door. She jumped. Most of her possessions were still packed away in boxes, so the knock had resulted in an echoing boom. She had no more than taken two steps when the knock sounded a second time.

"I'm coming," she called out. "Coming."

She was just about to open the door when she thought it might be better to first see who her visitor might be through the peephole instead. The breezeway on the other side of the door appeared empty.

Guess they had the wrong apartment, she thought, returning to her labor. She kneeled beside the box of ornaments and pulled out a figurine of a dancing girl her grandmother had gifted her on her sixteenth birthday. She held it up, loving how the light shining through the glass made patterns on the room's freshly installed carpets. Holding the figurine in her hand, she dug through the box, looking for its hook so she might hang it next to the apartment's kitchen window.

The boom of a heavy-handed knock on the door startled her again. She gently placed the dancer on the box and returned to the front door, but once again the breezeway on the other side appeared empty.

She pursed her lips. She'd seen several kids playing ball down the street the day before as she'd begun moving in. They must have played a prank on her. Opening the door a crack, she shouted, "go home."

Her eye caught the box of juice on the kitchen countertop. She frowned. She must have forgotten to put it away after making her drink earlier. She glanced back at the door and shrugged. "Why not?" She poured herself a second drink that was more champagne than juice and raised her glass. "Here's to the next chapter," she said out loud. She tipped the glass back and draining its contents. The combination of pulp and bubbles tickled her tongue.

She took a step toward the main room and bumped into the wall. She giggled. "I made that drink too strong."

She stepped on the carpet, loving how its plush weave surrounded her toes. Another round of knocking boomed from the front door, this time even louder and more insistent. She turned her head and shouted, "go away, whoever you are." Her ears detected the sound of a siren in the distance. Good, she thought, maybe someone else got tired of those kids and called in a complaint.

She returned to the box of ornaments. The room began to spin. Yeah, that drink was way too strong. Lesson learned. She sat down in an attempt to reclaim her equilibrium, but the dizziness increased. She looked for something to center her gaze on.

Only then did she realize the figurine was gone.

An Average Day in the life of Matt Summers

FIRST PUBLISHED FEBRUARY 21, 2019

Matt Summers lived in an average house on an average street where nothing ever happened.

His mother would wake him by opening his curtains, allowing the light to stream in. Only today, his mother snapped them shut shortly after opening them.

"Wha's going on?" asked a bleary-eyed Matt.

"Oh nothing," said his mother. "I just realized that it's Saturday and thought you could use a little extra rest this morning. I couldn't help but notice how much you're still growing."

Matt smiled. He had every intention of burrowing back under his covers, but then remembered how close he'd come to beating level twelve on his favorite video game the day before. Unable to go back to sleep, he slid off the bed and padded into the den where he found his mother pulling a decorative sword off the wall. "What'cha doing?" he asked.

"Just pulling this down to give it a cleaning," said his mother after a slight pause. "I noticed a bit of tarnish." She tittered, though whatever the joke was, it went over

Matt's head. "Er. Why don't you go and get yourself a bit of breakfast?"

Matt nodded and entered the kitchen where he poured himself a bowl of cereal. His father entered the room. "Have you seen your mother?" he asked.

"She's in the den," Matt said, spilling a bit of milk on the counter. "Acting weird. Taking the sword off the wall so she can polish it."

"Ah," said his father, his face taking on a severe expression.

Matt looked at the spot of milk on the counter. "Don't worry, I'll clean that up."

His father blinked. "Right. I'll go see if I can help your mother." He turned and exited the room, leaving Matt to finish his breakfast in peace.

After shoveling the cereal into his mouth, Matt went into the den and fired up his video game console. His dad re-appeared, briefly holding a large dusty leather-bound book. Matt guessed his mother must have found another cleaning project for his father to do. "You're blocking the screen," said Matt.

His father started. "Sorry," he said "I must have been distracted. Didn't see you there." before exiting the room in the direction of the front door.

The game's intro music blasted over the speakers. "Alright," said Matt to himself. "Let's do this thing."

Several hours later, Matt jumped around the room. He'd done it. Not only had he beaten level twelve, he'd defeated the baddie on level thirteen and fourteen too. He couldn't wait to tell his friend, Oscar, on Monday all about it. The game's sound designers had really pulled out all the stops on level thirteen. At times, it had seemed as if the sound of explosions were coming from outside of his house rather than on the small screen in front of him. However, the game designers must have spent their entire budget on level thirteen as fourteen had sounded dull and dead by comparison outside of a single, solitary crash.

His stomach rumbled realizing he'd played his game well past lunch. On his way to the pantry, he noticed the trashcan was full. His mouth twisted and his nose wrinkled, but he grabbed the sack. The garbage was his responsibility and his mom was obviously in one of her whole house cleaning moods. If he didn't take the initiative to take it out to the curb on his own, he knew from experience more chores would follow.

Outside, the air smelled of smoke. One of the neighbors must be smoking a pork shoulder. There was something else, though Matt couldn't quite place it. It was like eggs and milk gone bad. He glanced at the bag of garbage he held in one hand. The stench was probably from that, he just hadn't noticed it inside.

Rounding the corner, he found his father leaning against the home's brick wall. "Taking a break?" Matt asked.

"I guess you can say that," said his dad, picking up the book from where it lay on the ground, still as dusty as it had earlier that day.

"You got something on your shirt," said Matt pointing at a large oily-looking stain.

His father looked down. "So I do," he said. "I should probably go and get this cleaned up before it sets." His father then turned and went inside taking the book with him.

Matt spotted the little old woman who lived at the end of the street standing in the middle of the road. She was staring at their house. He waved. The woman scowled and scurried away. Matt shrugged and returned inside where he found his mother re-attaching the freshly cleaned blade to its place on the wall.

"Sorry, sweetie," she said noticing him there. "That took longer than I thought it would."

"That's okay, mom," he said, picking up his controller and returning to his game, which he played through dinner. Later that night, Matt lay on his average-sized bed, in his average-sized room feeling he'd accomplished a lot, and yet at the same time, it was as if he had missed something more. He turned over on his side. Giving into dreams, he let the feeling go. After all, it had been just another day on a street where nothing ever happened.

Nikki Kan't Quit

FIRST PUBLISHED NOVEMBER 1 2018

Nikki Kant drummed her fingers on her desk's cheap veneer while she listened to the city liaison ramble on her voicemail. The desk was one of those cheap particle board models you order over the internet and assemble yourself and had a tendency to wobble if her daily paperwork and personal clutter wasn't placed on its surface just right. The vibration from her finger's impact sent a pen rolling off its edge. She didn't bother to pick it up.

The liaison's voice increased in volume, becoming more clipped by the second as he worked himself into a rage. Apparently, helping a friend was the sort of thing that was frowned upon in the eyes of the city. She'd heard enough. Returning the outdated handset to its cradle, she pulled out a desk drawer. Her fingers paused over the accordion folder that hid her secret stash of dark chocolate covered caramel seasoned with sea salt. I'm going to need this. She pulled out the accordion folder out as well as a second file folder.

The drawer stuck when she tried to shove it close. Nikki tried again. The drawer remained firmly in its position. Figures, she thought. Folders in hand, Nikki walked over to her boss' office. By the look of his expression through the glass window, he was off to a similar morning. She tapped on the door with her knuckle before letting herself in without waiting for him to wave.

"Chief."

"Do you realize I've had five reporters call me already?" He glanced at the clock hanging on the wall over her head. "It's not even nine." His desk phone rang. The chief frowned. "I'm guessing that's another one now. Do you want to explain what you were thinking?"

"Not particularly, no. It shouldn't matter. I was off duty."

"Off duty or not, what you do reflects on this department. I hope you understand how serious this situation is."

"I don't, actually. All I did was go for a run."

"That's not all you did, and you and I both know it."

Nikki shrugged.

The chief stood and placed his hands on his desk. "You're on your way to a suspension pending a full investigation into your behavior over the last few weeks—you understand that, don't you?"

"That won't be necessary, sir," said Nikki, separating the accordion holding her stash from the second folder containing a single sheet of paper.

The chief's eyebrow shot up. "You're quitting?" He sat back in his chair. It creaked under his weight. "I have to admit, I'm a little disappointed. I thought it would take more to break you."

Nikki snorted. She opened the thin folder and pulled out its contents. "I'm anything but broken," she said placing the resignation letter on his desk. "I suggest you read it." She tucked the accordion folder under her arm. She wasn't going to need reinforcements after all. Finally going through with her decision after drafting the letter days ago felt better than eating a dozen chocolate bars.

The chief stared at the piece of paper. "This changes nothing," he said.

"Oh, I'm pretty sure it changes everything." She removed the badge from her breast and placed it on the desk next to her resignation letter.

"You walk out that door, and you're on your own. I won't be able to protect you anymore."

Nikki smiled. "I survived three tours. I think I can manage."

A brief knock on the door announced their meeting. Rangle poked his head in. "Chief, I just heard-" He noticed Nikki's presence, then his gaze moved to the chief's desk. He couldn't have missed the badge nor the sheet of paper. "I knew it," he said. "I pegged you as a quitter your first day."

"That's surprising," said Nikki. "Considering you've always been a terrible detective."

Rangle's face took on a shade of puce. He turned to the chief. "So, as I was saying, I just heard that we got a lead on that bomb threat last week."

"It's a distraction," said Nikki. "If either of you had only listened—"

"That's enough, Ms. Kant." The chief slammed his palm down on the desk. "You've made your decision." He nodded at her resignation letter. "Now, how about you get out of my office so the rest of us can do the job you're walking away from."

I'm not walking away from anything, she thought. She turned on her heel and opened the office door. I'm just not following your rules anymore. She closed the door with a bang. A few of the other officers lingering nearby glanced her way at the sound, but no one stopped her as she made her way past the main desk and out the door. Nikki smiled. It was just as well. They wouldn't have been able to stop her now, even if they'd tried.

Acknowledgments

There are very few pages as intimidating as a blank page. You would think that wouldn't be the case for a writer. After all, we make it our business to slay blank pages on a daily basis. Unfortunately, even dragon slayers need to coach the beast out of its cave to do their job.

When I decided I wanted to be an author, I was told that to be seen as a legitimate professional, I needed a website. Alliepottswrites.com was born. However, while it was easy enough to register for a domain and throw up a page with my book details on it, it figuring out what else to post proved a challenge. The experts will tell you to write about what you know.

I can tell you a lot about television shows aired back before we had streaming services. I can go on for hours discussing the evolution of the epic fantasy novel and the authors who influenced me. I can make a person nervously look toward the door and make hasty excuses to leave while I go on and on about technology or science. I can't, however, tell you how many times the subject of poop has come up at a dinner conversation. I lost count years ago.

In the end, I decided I would try blogging and used my website to share my journey. After all, while I know a number of things, the one thing I consider myself a true expert on is my life. This book is a compilation of my favorite posts from the blog, and couldn't have been written if it were not for my family's various antics or without reading the various writing prompts provided by other generous writers too numerous to name individually.

That said, I do want to thank my mom for helping me with much of the initial grunt work required to pull this collection together. If, after reading this book, anyone comes away with the opinion I am a good mom, it is because I learned from the best. And if not, they can blame dad.

If you liked what you've read, please consider leaving a review on your favorite online retail site (and tell a friend). Reviews help guide readers, but they also increase the chance a book will appear in the search results on these sites in the first place.

You can also sign-up to receive more content like this book by subscribing to my email list at:

http://eepurl.com/c0fcSj.

About the Author

Allie Potts, born in Rochester Minnesota, was moved to North Carolina at a very early age by parents eager to escape to a more forgiving climate. She has since continued to call North Carolina home, settling in Raleigh, halfway between the mountains and the sea, in 1998.

When not finding ways to squeeze in 72 hours into a 24 day or chasing after children determined to turn her hair gray before its time, Allie enjoys stories of all kinds. Her favorites, whether they are novels, film, or simply shared aloud with friends, are usually accompanied with a glass of wine or cup of coffee in hand.

A self-professed science geek and book nerd, Allie also writes at www.alliepottswrites.com.

want to connect?

Email Allie at: allie@alliepottswrites.com
Facebook: https://www.facebook.com/alliepottswrites
Twitter: @alliepottswrite
Pinterest: @alliepottswrite
Instagram: @alliepottswrites
Bookbub: https://www.bookbub.com/profile/allie-potts

Other Titles by Allie Potts

PROJECT GENE ASSIST

Ready or not, the next era of human evolution is here

The Fair & Foul
The Watch & Wand
Lies & Legacy

ROCKY ROW NOVELS

Living happily ever after is a full-time job

An Uncertain Faith
An Uncertain Confidence

www.ingramcontent.com/pod-product-compliance
Lightning Source LLC
Chambersburg PA
CBHW030435010526
44118CB00011B/638